CERTIFIED ETHICAL HACKER

RECONNAISSANCE, VULNERABILITY ANALYSIS & SOCIAL ENGINEERING

3 BOOKS IN 1

BOOK 1
CERTIFIED ETHICAL HACKER: FOUNDATIONS OF RECONNAISSANCE TECHNIQUES

BOOK 2
CERTIFIED ETHICAL HACKER: ADVANCED VULNERABILITY ANALYSIS STRATEGIES

BOOK 3
CERTIFIED ETHICAL HACKER: MASTERING SOCIAL ENGINEERING TACTICS

ROB BOTWRIGHT

Published by Rob Botwright
Library of Congress Cataloging-in-Publication Data
ISBN 978-1-83938-797-5
Cover design by Rizzo

Disclaimer

The contents of this book are based on extensive research and the best available historical sources. However, the author and publisher make no claims, promises, or guarantees about the accuracy, completeness, or adequacy of the information contained herein. The information in this book is provided on an "as is" basis, and the author and publisher disclaim any and all liability for any errors, omissions, or inaccuracies in the information or for any actions taken in reliance on such information. The opinions and views expressed in this book are those of the author and do not necessarily reflect the official policy or position of any organization or individual mentioned in this book. Any reference to specific people, places, or events is intended only to provide historical context and is not intended to defame or malign any group, individual, or entity. The information in this book is intended for educational and entertainment purposes only. It is not intended to be a substitute for professional advice or judgment. Readers are encouraged to conduct their own research and to seek professional advice where appropriate. Every effort has been made to obtain necessary permissions and acknowledgments for all images and other copyrighted material used in this book. Any errors or omissions in this regard are unintentional, and the author and publisher will correct them in future editions.

BOOK 1 - CERTIFIED ETHICAL HACKER: FOUNDATIONS OF RECONNAISSANCE TECHNIQUES

BOOK 2 - CERTIFIED ETHICAL HACKER: ADVANCED VULNERABILITY ANALYSIS STRATEGIES

BOOK 3 - CERTIFIED ETHICAL HACKER: MASTERING SOCIAL ENGINEERING TACTICS

Introduction

Welcome to the "Certified Ethical Hacker: Reconnaissance, Vulnerability Analysis & Social Engineering" book bundle, a comprehensive collection designed to equip readers with the essential knowledge and practical skills required to navigate the intricate landscape of ethical hacking. In today's interconnected world, cybersecurity threats continue to evolve, posing significant challenges to individuals and organizations alike. As such, there is a growing demand for skilled professionals who can proactively identify and mitigate these threats through ethical hacking practices.

This book bundle consists of three volumes, each focusing on a distinct aspect of ethical hacking:

Book 1 - Certified Ethical Hacker: Foundations of Reconnaissance Techniques:

In this volume, readers will embark on a journey through the fundamentals of reconnaissance, the critical first step in any ethical hacking endeavor. From passive information gathering to active reconnaissance techniques, readers will learn how to gather valuable intelligence about target systems and networks while adhering to ethical guidelines.

Book 2 - Certified Ethical Hacker: Advanced Vulnerability Analysis Strategies: Building upon the foundational knowledge acquired in the first volume, this book delves deeper into the realm of vulnerability analysis. Readers will explore advanced strategies for identifying, exploiting, and mitigating vulnerabilities in target systems, equipping them with the skills needed to conduct thorough security assessments and penetration tests.

Book 3 - Certified Ethical Hacker: Mastering Social Engineering Tactics: In the final volume of the bundle, readers will uncover the human element of cybersecurity through an exploration of social engineering tactics. From phishing and pretexting to vishing and impersonation, readers will learn how malicious actors manipulate human behavior to compromise security. By mastering these tactics, readers will be better prepared to defend against social engineering attacks and protect sensitive information.

Whether you are a cybersecurity professional looking to enhance your skills, a student aspiring to enter the field, or an individual interested in learning about ethical hacking, this book bundle offers a comprehensive and practical resource. Each volume is packed with hands-on exercises, real-world examples, and actionable insights, providing readers with the knowledge and tools needed to succeed in the dynamic world of cybersecurity.

Join us on this journey as we explore the intricacies of ethical hacking, from reconnaissance and vulnerability analysis to social engineering tactics. Together, let us empower ourselves to defend against cyber threats and safeguard the digital world.

BOOK 1

CERTIFIED ETHICAL HACKER FOUNDATIONS OF RECONNAISSANCE TECHNIQUES

ROB BOTWRIGHT

Chapter 1: Introduction to Cybersecurity Fundamentals

Understanding the basics of information security is crucial in today's digital landscape where threats to data integrity and confidentiality abound, from malicious hackers seeking unauthorized access to sensitive information to inadvertent data breaches caused by human error or technical vulnerabilities, a robust foundation in information security principles is essential for individuals and organizations alike to safeguard their digital assets and maintain trust with stakeholders, at its core, information security encompasses a broad range of concepts and practices designed to protect the confidentiality, integrity, and availability of information assets, whether they are stored, processed, or transmitted electronically, one of the fundamental principles of information security is the CIA triad, which stands for confidentiality, integrity, and availability, these three principles form the cornerstone of effective information security management, confidentiality refers to the assurance that sensitive information is only accessible to authorized individuals or entities, ensuring that data remains confidential requires implementing strong access controls, encryption, and other security measures to prevent unauthorized disclosure, integrity ensures that information remains accurate, complete, and unaltered during storage, processing, or transmission, protecting data integrity involves implementing measures such as data validation, checksums, and digital signatures to detect and prevent unauthorized modifications, availability ensures that information is accessible and usable when needed by authorized users, safeguarding data availability involves implementing redundancy, backups, and disaster recovery plans to mitigate the impact of disruptions or outages, in addition to the CIA triad, information security also encompasses other key concepts such as authentication, authorization, and accountability, authentication verifies the identity of users or systems, typically through the use of passwords, biometrics, or cryptographic tokens, authorization determines what actions users are allowed to perform based on their authenticated identity and assigned permissions, accountability ensures that actions taken by users can be traced back to their individual identities, facilitating accountability requires implementing logging, auditing, and monitoring mechanisms to track user activities and detect unauthorized or suspicious behavior, another important aspect of information security is risk management, which involves identifying, assessing, and mitigating risks to information assets, risk management helps organizations prioritize their security efforts and allocate resources effectively to address the most significant threats and vulnerabilities, implementing an effective risk management program requires conducting risk assessments, developing risk mitigation strategies, and regularly reviewing and updating security controls, in addition to technical measures, information security also relies on policies, procedures, and training to ensure that employees understand their roles and responsibilities in protecting sensitive information, establishing clear security policies and procedures helps to promote consistency and compliance with regulatory requirements, while ongoing training and awareness programs help to educate employees about security best practices and reduce the likelihood of security incidents caused by human error or negligence, in summary, understanding the basics of information security is essential for individuals and organizations to protect their digital assets and mitigate the risks of cyber threats, by implementing sound security practices, including the CIA triad, authentication, authorization, accountability, risk management, and security policies and training, organizations can enhance their resilience to cyber attacks and maintain trust with stakeholders. Understanding the importance of cybersecurity awareness is paramount in today's interconnected digital world, where individuals and organizations face an ever-evolving landscape of cyber threats and vulnerabilities, cybersecurity awareness encompasses the knowledge, attitudes, and behaviors necessary to protect oneself and others from cyber attacks and security breaches, at its core, cybersecurity awareness involves recognizing potential risks, understanding best practices for mitigating those risks, and taking proactive steps to secure digital assets and information, one of the primary reasons why cybersecurity awareness is so crucial is the increasing prevalence of cyber attacks targeting individuals, businesses, and governments, from phishing scams and ransomware attacks to data breaches and identity theft, cyber threats pose significant risks to personal privacy, financial security, and national security, raising awareness about these threats helps individuals and organizations recognize warning signs and take appropriate precautions to defend against them, in addition to protecting against external threats, cybersecurity awareness also helps to mitigate insider threats, which can be caused by employees, contractors, or other trusted individuals with access to sensitive information or systems, by educating employees about the importance of data security and the potential consequences of negligent or malicious behavior, organizations can reduce the likelihood of insider incidents and safeguard their assets, another reason why cybersecurity awareness is essential is the growing reliance on digital technologies in both personal and professional contexts, from online banking and shopping to remote work and cloud computing, digital technologies have transformed the way we live and work, providing unprecedented convenience and efficiency but also introducing new risks and vulnerabilities, raising awareness about cybersecurity helps individuals make informed decisions about their online activities and adopt security best practices to protect themselves and their devices from cyber threats, furthermore, cybersecurity awareness is essential for promoting a culture of security within organizations, where employees understand their roles and responsibilities in safeguarding sensitive information and maintaining compliance with security policies and regulations, by fostering a culture of security, organizations can create a collaborative environment where everyone takes ownership of cybersecurity and works together to identify and mitigate risks, in addition to educating employees, cybersecurity awareness also involves engaging with the broader community to promote digital literacy and responsible online behavior, this includes partnering with schools, libraries, and community organizations to deliver cybersecurity training and resources to individuals of all ages and backgrounds, by empowering people with the knowledge and skills they need to protect themselves online, we can create a safer and more secure digital ecosystem for everyone, deploying cybersecurity awareness initiatives requires a multifaceted approach that combines education, training, and outreach efforts, organizations can offer cybersecurity awareness training to employees through online courses, workshops, and seminars covering topics such as password security, phishing awareness, and safe browsing habits, they can also provide resources such as cybersecurity awareness posters, infographics, and tip sheets to reinforce key messages and promote good security practices, in addition to formal training programs, organizations can raise awareness about cybersecurity through ongoing communication and engagement efforts, this may include sending out regular security reminders, sharing news and updates about emerging threats, and promoting cybersecurity events and activities, by keeping cybersecurity top of mind and encouraging open dialogue about security concerns, organizations can create a culture of vigilance where everyone plays a role in protecting against cyber threats, ultimately, the importance of cybersecurity awareness cannot be overstated in today's digital age, where the stakes are higher than ever before, by educating ourselves and others about the risks and best practices for staying safe online, we can reduce our vulnerability to cyber attacks and build a more resilient and secure digital future.

Chapter 2: Understanding Reconnaissance in Ethical Hacking

Understanding reconnaissance objectives and goals is essential in the realm of cybersecurity, as reconnaissance serves as the crucial first step in any successful attack, whether conducted by malicious hackers or ethical hackers seeking to identify vulnerabilities and strengthen defenses, at its core, reconnaissance involves gathering information about a target system, network, or organization to identify potential weaknesses and opportunities for exploitation, by understanding the objectives and goals of reconnaissance, cybersecurity professionals can develop effective strategies for defending against cyber threats and minimizing the risk of security breaches, one of the primary objectives of reconnaissance is to gather information about the target's infrastructure, including its network architecture, system configurations, and software applications, this information helps attackers identify potential entry points and vulnerabilities that can be exploited to gain unauthorized access, to achieve this objective, attackers may use a variety of techniques, such as network scanning, port scanning, and service enumeration, to map out the target's digital footprint and identify potential attack vectors, for example, the 'nmap' command can be used to conduct a port scan of a target network, revealing open ports and services that may be vulnerable to exploitation, another objective of reconnaissance is to gather information about the target's employees, partners, and customers, this information can include names, email addresses, job titles, and organizational roles, which attackers can use to craft targeted phishing emails or social engineering attacks, to achieve this objective, attackers may use techniques such as OSINT (Open Source Intelligence) gathering, which involves collecting publicly available information from sources such as social media, company websites, and online forums, for example, tools like 'theHarvester' can be used to automate the collection of email addresses and other information from public sources, yet another objective of reconnaissance is to identify potential security controls and defenses that may be in place, such as firewalls, intrusion detection systems, and antivirus software, understanding the target's security posture helps attackers assess the likelihood of success for their attacks and determine the best course of action, to achieve this objective, attackers may use techniques such as banner grabbing, which involves collecting information from network banners and service banners to identify specific software versions and configurations, for example, the 'telnet' or 'nc' command can be used to connect to a target system and retrieve banner information from open ports, overall, the objectives and goals of reconnaissance are to gather information, identify vulnerabilities, and assess the target's security posture to facilitate successful attacks, by understanding these objectives, cybersecurity professionals can develop proactive defenses and security measures to protect against reconnaissance activities and mitigate the risk of cyber attacks. Understanding the various types of reconnaissance activities is crucial in the field of cybersecurity, as reconnaissance serves as the foundation for successful attacks by providing attackers with the information they need to identify vulnerabilities and exploit weaknesses in a target's defenses, reconnaissance activities can be broadly categorized into two main types: passive reconnaissance and active reconnaissance, passive reconnaissance involves gathering information about a target without directly interacting with it, making it difficult for defenders to detect or block, one common method of passive reconnaissance is passive network reconnaissance, which involves monitoring network traffic to collect information about devices, services, and protocols, passive network reconnaissance can be conducted using tools such as Wireshark, tcpdump, or Zeek (formerly known as Bro), which capture and analyze network packets to identify hosts, open ports, and other network attributes, another type of passive reconnaissance is passive DNS reconnaissance, which involves querying DNS servers for information about a target's domain names and subdomains, passive DNS reconnaissance can be conducted using tools such as dnSpy or PassiveTotal, which aggregate and analyze passive DNS data from multiple sources, in addition to passive reconnaissance, attackers may also conduct active reconnaissance activities to gather information about a target by directly interacting with it, one common method of active reconnaissance is port scanning, which involves sending probe packets to a target's IP addresses and analyzing the responses to identify open ports and services, port scanning can be conducted using tools such as Nmap, Masscan, or Zmap, which automate the process of sending probe packets and analyzing responses, another type of active reconnaissance is network mapping, which involves creating a map of a target's network infrastructure to identify hosts, subnets, and network devices, network mapping can be conducted using tools such as NetMapper, OpenVAS, or Nessus, which scan the target's network and generate maps showing the relationships between hosts and devices, yet another type of active reconnaissance is vulnerability scanning, which involves scanning a target's systems and applications for known vulnerabilities that can be exploited to gain unauthorized access, vulnerability scanning can be conducted using tools such as OpenVAS, Nessus, or Qualys, which scan the target's network and identify vulnerabilities based on known signatures and patterns, in addition to these common types of reconnaissance activities, attackers may also use more advanced techniques such as social engineering, which involves manipulating individuals into divulging sensitive information or performing actions that compromise security, social engineering can take many forms, including phishing emails, pretexting phone calls, or physical tailgating, to defend against reconnaissance activities, organizations can implement a variety of security measures, such as network segmentation, intrusion detection systems, and access controls, which restrict unauthorized access to sensitive information and resources, by understanding the different types of reconnaissance activities and implementing effective security measures, organizations can reduce their exposure to cyber threats and protect their digital assets from attack.

Chapter 3: Passive Information Gathering Methods

Passive reconnaissance, an essential phase in the reconnaissance process, involves collecting information about a target without direct interaction or probing, distinguishing itself from active reconnaissance by its stealthy and non-intrusive nature, passive reconnaissance allows attackers to gather valuable intelligence while minimizing the risk of detection, making it an attractive strategy for both malicious hackers and ethical hackers alike, the primary goal of passive reconnaissance is to gather information about a target's systems, networks, and employees without alerting defenders to the attacker's presence, one common method of passive reconnaissance is passive network reconnaissance, which involves monitoring network traffic to collect information about hosts, services, and protocols, passive network reconnaissance can be accomplished using tools such as Wireshark, tcpdump, or Zeek (formerly known as Bro), which capture and analyze network packets to identify hosts, open ports, and other network attributes, by passively observing network traffic, attackers can gain insights into a target's infrastructure and identify potential vulnerabilities that can be exploited in later stages of an attack, another method of passive reconnaissance is passive DNS reconnaissance, which involves querying DNS servers for information about a target's domain names and subdomains, passive DNS reconnaissance can reveal valuable information such as domain ownership, domain registration details, and DNS records, attackers can use this information to identify potential targets for further reconnaissance or exploitation, passive DNS reconnaissance can be conducted using tools such as dnSpy or PassiveTotal, which aggregate and analyze passive DNS data from multiple sources, in addition to network reconnaissance, attackers may also conduct passive reconnaissance on other digital assets, such as websites, social media accounts, and online forums, one common method of passive reconnaissance on websites is web crawling, which involves systematically browsing a website to collect information about its structure, content, and functionality, web crawling can be performed using tools such as wget, curl, or HTTrack, which recursively download web pages and parse HTML to extract links, images, and other resources, by analyzing the structure and content of a website, attackers can gain insights into its architecture, technology stack, and potential vulnerabilities, another method of passive reconnaissance is passive reconnaissance on social media, which involves monitoring social media platforms for information about a target's employees, partners, and customers, attackers can use this information to craft targeted phishing emails or social engineering attacks, passive reconnaissance on social media can be conducted using manual techniques or automated tools that scrape social media profiles and analyze publicly available information, by passively collecting information from various sources, attackers can gain a comprehensive understanding of their target's digital footprint and identify potential weaknesses that can be exploited in future attacks, to defend against passive reconnaissance, organizations can implement a variety of security measures, such as network monitoring, encryption, and access controls, which restrict unauthorized access to sensitive information and resources, by understanding the methods and techniques used in passive reconnaissance and implementing effective security measures, organizations can reduce their exposure to cyber threats and protect their digital assets from attack. Data collection techniques without active engagement, also known as passive data collection methods, play a crucial role in reconnaissance activities by allowing attackers to gather information about a target without directly interacting with it, these techniques are particularly valuable for attackers seeking to minimize their footprint and avoid detection while gathering intelligence about their target, one common passive data collection method is passive network reconnaissance, which involves monitoring network traffic to collect information about hosts, services, and protocols, this can be achieved using tools such as Wireshark, tcpdump, or Zeek (formerly known as Bro), which capture and analyze network packets to identify hosts, open ports, and other network attributes, by passively observing network traffic, attackers can gain insights into a target's infrastructure and identify potential vulnerabilities that can be exploited in later stages of an attack, another passive data collection method is passive DNS reconnaissance, which involves querying DNS servers for information about a target's domain names and subdomains, passive DNS reconnaissance can reveal valuable information such as domain ownership, registration details, and DNS records, attackers can use this information to identify potential targets for further reconnaissance or exploitation, passive DNS reconnaissance can be conducted using tools such as dnSpy or PassiveTotal, which aggregate and analyze passive DNS data from multiple sources, in addition to network reconnaissance, attackers may also conduct passive reconnaissance on other digital assets, such as websites, social media accounts, and online forums, one common method of passive reconnaissance on websites is web crawling, which involves systematically browsing a website to collect information about its structure, content, and functionality, web crawling can be performed using tools such as wget, curl, or HTTrack, which recursively download web pages and parse HTML to extract links, images, and other resources, by analyzing the structure and content of a website, attackers can gain insights into its architecture, technology stack, and potential vulnerabilities, another passive data collection method is passive reconnaissance on social media, which involves monitoring social media platforms for information about a target's employees, partners, and customers, attackers can use this information to craft targeted phishing emails or social engineering attacks, passive reconnaissance on social media can be conducted using manual techniques or automated tools that scrape social media profiles and analyze publicly available information, by passively collecting information from various sources, attackers can gain a comprehensive understanding of their target's digital footprint and identify potential weaknesses that can be exploited in future attacks, to defend against passive data collection techniques, organizations can implement a variety of security measures, such as network monitoring, encryption, and access controls, which restrict unauthorized access to sensitive information and resources, by understanding the methods and techniques used in passive data collection and implementing effective security measures, organizations can reduce their exposure to cyber threats and protect their digital assets from attack.

Chapter 4: Active Information Gathering Techniques

Active reconnaissance, a critical phase in the reconnaissance process, involves directly interacting with a target to gather information about its systems, networks, and employees, unlike passive reconnaissance, which focuses on collecting information without alerting the target, active reconnaissance requires attackers to send probe packets or conduct scans that may be detected by defensive measures such as intrusion detection systems or firewalls, despite the increased risk of detection, active reconnaissance provides attackers with real-time information about a target's vulnerabilities and weaknesses, making it an essential component of the attack lifecycle, one common method of active reconnaissance is port scanning, which involves sending probe packets to a target's IP addresses and analyzing the responses to identify open ports and services, port scanning can be conducted using tools such as Nmap, Masscan, or Zmap, which automate the process of sending probe packets and analyzing responses, by identifying open ports and services, attackers can gain insights into the target's network architecture and potential attack vectors, another method of active reconnaissance is network mapping, which involves creating a map of a target's network infrastructure to identify hosts, subnets, and network devices, network mapping can be conducted using tools such as NetMapper, OpenVAS, or Nessus, which scan the target's network and generate maps showing the relationships between hosts and devices, by visualizing the target's network topology, attackers can identify critical assets and prioritize their attack efforts, yet another method of active reconnaissance is vulnerability scanning, which involves scanning a target's systems and applications for known vulnerabilities that can be exploited to gain unauthorized access, vulnerability scanning can be conducted using tools such as OpenVAS, Nessus, or Qualys, which scan the target's network and identify vulnerabilities based on known signatures and patterns, by identifying vulnerabilities, attackers can assess the target's security posture and determine the best course of action for launching their attacks, in addition to these common methods of active reconnaissance, attackers may also use more advanced techniques such as social engineering, which involves manipulating individuals into divulging sensitive information or performing actions that compromise security, social engineering can take many forms, including phishing emails, pretexting phone calls, or physical tailgating, to defend against active reconnaissance, organizations can implement a variety of security measures, such as intrusion detection systems, firewalls, and access controls, which detect and block suspicious activity on the network, by monitoring for signs of active reconnaissance, organizations can identify potential threats and take proactive steps to protect their digital assets, overall, active reconnaissance plays a crucial role in the reconnaissance process by providing attackers with real-time information about a target's vulnerabilities and weaknesses, while posing risks to the attacker in terms of detection, understanding the methods and techniques used in active reconnaissance and implementing effective security measures can help organizations reduce their exposure to cyber threats and protect their digital assets from attack. Tools and methods for active data collection play a crucial role in the reconnaissance phase of cybersecurity operations, enabling attackers to gather real-time information about their targets by directly interacting with them, one of the most commonly used tools for active data collection is Nmap, a powerful network scanning tool that allows attackers to discover hosts and services on a network, Nmap can be deployed using various command-line options, such as "nmap -sS" to perform a SYN scan or "nmap -Pn" to skip host discovery and proceed directly to port scanning, by scanning target networks with Nmap, attackers can identify open ports and services that may be vulnerable to exploitation, another tool commonly used for active data collection is Nessus, a vulnerability scanning tool that allows attackers to scan target systems and applications for known vulnerabilities, Nessus can be deployed using a web-based interface or command-line interface, with options such as "nessuscli scan" to initiate a vulnerability scan or "nessuscli report" to generate a report of scan results, by scanning target systems with Nessus, attackers can identify vulnerabilities that may be exploited to gain unauthorized access, yet another tool for active data collection is Metasploit, an exploitation framework that allows attackers to develop, test, and execute exploits against target systems, Metasploit can be deployed using a command-line interface or graphical user interface, with options such as "msfconsole" to launch the Metasploit console or "msfvenom" to generate custom payloads, by exploiting vulnerabilities with Metasploit, attackers can gain remote access to target systems and extract sensitive information, in addition to these tools, attackers may also use various methods for active data collection, such as social engineering, which involves manipulating individuals into divulging sensitive information or performing actions that compromise security, social engineering can take many forms, including phishing emails, pretexting phone calls, or physical tailgating, to defend against active data collection, organizations can implement a variety of security measures, such as intrusion detection systems, firewalls, and access controls, which detect and block suspicious activity on the network, by monitoring for signs of active data collection, organizations can identify potential threats and take proactive steps to protect their digital assets, overall, tools and methods for active data collection play a critical role in cybersecurity operations, enabling attackers to gather real-time information about their targets and identify vulnerabilities that may be exploited in subsequent stages of an attack, understanding the capabilities of these tools and methods, as well as implementing effective security measures, can help organizations reduce their exposure to cyber threats and protect their digital assets from attack.

Chapter 5: Footprinting and Fingerprinting: Profiling the Target

Footprinting techniques and tools are essential components of the reconnaissance phase in cybersecurity, enabling attackers to gather information about their targets and identify potential vulnerabilities, footprinting involves systematically gathering information about a target's networks, systems, and employees to gain insights into its digital footprint and security posture, one common footprinting technique is passive reconnaissance, which involves collecting information about a target without directly interacting with it, passive reconnaissance can include methods such as DNS interrogation, which involves querying DNS servers for information about a target's domain names and subdomains, attackers can use tools like 'nslookup' or 'dig' to perform DNS interrogation and retrieve information such as IP addresses, hostnames, and mail server records, another passive reconnaissance technique is network sniffing, which involves monitoring network traffic to collect information about hosts, services, and protocols, attackers can use tools like Wireshark or tcpdump to capture and analyze network packets, identifying hosts, open ports, and other network attributes, by passively observing network traffic, attackers can gain insights into a target's infrastructure and potential attack vectors, in addition to passive reconnaissance, attackers may also use active reconnaissance techniques to gather information about their targets, one common active reconnaissance technique is port scanning, which involves sending probe packets to a target's IP addresses and analyzing the responses to identify open ports and services, attackers can use tools like Nmap or Masscan to conduct port scans, specifying options such as '-sS' for a SYN scan or '-sT' for a TCP connect scan, by identifying open ports and services, attackers can identify potential entry points and vulnerabilities that may be exploited in later stages of an attack, another active reconnaissance technique is network mapping, which involves creating a map of a target's network infrastructure to identify hosts, subnets, and network devices, attackers can use tools like NetMapper or Nmap to conduct network mapping scans, generating maps showing the relationships between hosts and devices, by visualizing the target's network topology, attackers can identify critical assets and prioritize their attack efforts, yet another active reconnaissance technique is social engineering, which involves manipulating individuals into divulging sensitive information or performing actions that compromise security, social engineering can take many forms, including phishing emails, pretexting phone calls, or physical tailgating, attackers can use tools like SET (Social Engineering Toolkit) or BeEF (Browser Exploitation Framework) to conduct social engineering attacks, crafting convincing emails or messages designed to trick recipients into revealing passwords or other sensitive information, by leveraging both passive and active reconnaissance techniques, attackers can gather comprehensive information about their targets and identify potential vulnerabilities that may be exploited in subsequent stages of an attack, to defend against footprinting techniques and tools, organizations can implement a variety of security measures, such as intrusion detection systems, firewalls, and access controls, which detect and block suspicious activity on the network, by monitoring for signs of footprinting activity, organizations can identify potential threats and take proactive steps to protect their digital assets, overall, understanding the capabilities of footprinting techniques and tools, as well as implementing effective security measures, is essential for organizations to defend against cyber threats and protect their digital assets from attack. Fingerprinting methods for target profiling are crucial elements in the reconnaissance phase of cybersecurity operations, allowing attackers to gather detailed information about their targets' systems, networks, and applications, by analyzing this information, attackers can identify vulnerabilities and potential points of entry for exploitation, one common fingerprinting method is banner grabbing, which involves connecting to a target system and retrieving information from banners or headers returned by servers, attackers can use tools like 'telnet' or 'nc' to manually connect to a target system and retrieve banners from open ports, such as 'telnet target_ip port' or 'nc -v target_ip port', by analyzing banners, attackers can identify specific software versions and configurations, helping them identify potential vulnerabilities that may be exploited, another fingerprinting method is protocol analysis, which involves analyzing network traffic to identify protocols and services running on a target's network, attackers can use tools like Wireshark or tcpdump to capture and analyze network packets, identifying protocols and services based on packet headers and payload data, by analyzing network traffic, attackers can gain insights into a target's network architecture and potential attack vectors, yet another fingerprinting method is operating system fingerprinting, which involves identifying the operating system running on a target system, attackers can use tools like Nmap or P0f to conduct operating system fingerprinting scans, specifying options such as '-O' for operating system detection or '-A' for advanced detection, by analyzing responses from target systems, attackers can identify unique characteristics and behaviors that can be used to determine the operating system running on the target, another fingerprinting method is application fingerprinting, which involves identifying specific applications and services running on a target system, attackers can use tools like Nmap or Netcat to conduct application fingerprinting scans, specifying options such as '-sV' for service version detection or '-p-' to scan all ports, by analyzing responses from target systems, attackers can identify specific applications and services, along with their versions and configurations, helping them identify potential vulnerabilities that may be exploited, yet another fingerprinting method is packet timing analysis, which involves analyzing the timing of packets sent and received during communication with a target system, attackers can use tools like Hping or Nping to conduct packet timing analysis scans, specifying options such as '--scanflags' to specify TCP flags or '--icmp-type' to specify ICMP packet types, by analyzing packet timing, attackers can gain insights into a target's network latency and responsiveness, which can be used to infer information about network topology and infrastructure, in addition to these fingerprinting methods, attackers may also use passive fingerprinting techniques, such as passive OS fingerprinting, which involves analyzing patterns of network traffic to infer information about target systems, attackers can use tools like P0f or PassiveTotal to conduct passive OS fingerprinting, analyzing network traffic patterns to identify operating systems and applications running on target systems, by leveraging a combination of active and passive fingerprinting methods, attackers can gather comprehensive information about their targets' systems, networks, and applications, helping them identify potential vulnerabilities and points of entry for exploitation, to defend against fingerprinting techniques, organizations can implement a variety of security measures, such as intrusion detection systems, firewalls, and network segmentation, which detect and block suspicious activity on the network, by monitoring for signs of fingerprinting activity, organizations can identify potential threats and take proactive steps to protect their digital assets from attack, overall, understanding the capabilities of fingerprinting methods and implementing effective security measures is essential for organizations to defend against cyber threats and protect their digital assets from exploitation.

Chapter 6: Google Hacking and Search Engine Reconnaissance

Leveraging search engines for reconnaissance is a fundamental aspect of information gathering in cybersecurity operations, as search engines index a vast amount of information about websites, domains, and online content, making them valuable tools for attackers seeking to gather intelligence about their targets, one common technique for leveraging search engines is Google hacking, which involves using advanced search operators to refine search queries and uncover sensitive information, attackers can use search operators such as "site:" to search within a specific domain or website, "intitle:" to search for specific words or phrases in the title of web pages, and "filetype:" to search for specific file types, by combining these operators with keywords related to their target, attackers can uncover information such as confidential documents, login pages, or exposed databases, for example, the command "site:example.com intitle:login" can be used to search for login pages within the example.com domain, revealing potential entry points for exploitation, another technique for leveraging search engines is OSINT (Open Source Intelligence) gathering, which involves using search engines to collect publicly available information about a target, attackers can use search engines to find information such as email addresses, social media profiles, company websites, and online forums, by analyzing this information, attackers can gain insights into their target's employees, partners, and customers, helping them craft targeted phishing emails or social engineering attacks, in addition to Google hacking and OSINT gathering, attackers may also use search engines to identify vulnerabilities in their target's web applications, one common technique is searching for specific error messages or HTTP status codes that may indicate potential security flaws, attackers can use search engines to find websites that return error messages such as "SQL syntax error" or "index of /admin", which may indicate SQL injection vulnerabilities or exposed directories, by identifying these vulnerabilities, attackers can gain unauthorized access to sensitive information or compromise the security of their target's systems, in addition to these techniques, attackers may also use search engines to identify targets for exploitation, one common technique is searching for vulnerable devices or services using specific keywords, attackers can use search engines to find devices such as webcams, routers, or industrial control systems that are exposed to the internet without proper security measures, by identifying these vulnerable devices, attackers can gain unauthorized access or launch attacks such as DDoS (Distributed Denial of Service), in addition to identifying vulnerable devices, attackers may also use search engines to find targets for social engineering attacks, one common technique is searching for email addresses or phone numbers associated with specific organizations or industries, attackers can use search engines to find contact information for employees or executives, which can be used to craft convincing phishing emails or pretexting phone calls, by leveraging search engines for reconnaissance, attackers can gather valuable intelligence about their targets and identify potential vulnerabilities that may be exploited in subsequent stages of an attack, to defend against these reconnaissance techniques, organizations can implement a variety of security measures, such as web application firewalls, intrusion detection systems, and access controls, which detect and block suspicious activity on the network, by monitoring for signs of reconnaissance activity and implementing effective security measures, organizations can reduce their exposure to cyber threats and protect their digital assets from attack, overall, understanding the capabilities of search engines and implementing effective security measures is essential for organizations to defend against reconnaissance attacks and protect their digital assets from exploitation. Google hacking techniques and queries are powerful tools in the arsenal of both malicious hackers and cybersecurity professionals, leveraging the advanced search capabilities of Google to uncover sensitive information about a target, one common technique in Google hacking is the use of advanced search operators to refine search queries and uncover specific types of information, for example, the "site:" operator can be used to search within a specific domain or website, allowing attackers to focus their search on a target's online presence, the syntax for using the "site:" operator is "site:example.com", where "example.com" is replaced with the target domain or website, by combining the "site:" operator with keywords related to their target, attackers can uncover information such as confidential documents, login pages, or exposed databases, another useful operator is "intitle:", which allows attackers to search for specific words or phrases in the title of web pages, the syntax for using the "intitle:" operator is "intitle:keyword", where "keyword" is replaced with the word or phrase being searched for, attackers can use this operator to search for web pages containing keywords such as "login", "admin", or "confidential", which may indicate potential entry points for exploitation, yet another powerful operator is "filetype:", which allows attackers to search for specific file types, such as PDFs, spreadsheets, or configuration files, the syntax for using the "filetype:" operator is "filetype:extension", where "extension" is replaced with the file type being searched for, attackers can use this operator to search for files containing sensitive information, such as "passwords", "configurations", or "invoices", by combining these operators with keywords related to their target, attackers can uncover a wealth of information that may be useful in launching cyber attacks or conducting security assessments, for example, the command "site:example.com intitle:login filetype:pdf" can be used to search for PDF documents containing login pages within the example.com domain, revealing potential vulnerabilities that may be exploited, another technique in Google hacking is the use of predefined search queries, which are commonly known search strings that have been developed and shared within the cybersecurity community, these predefined search queries can be used to uncover specific types of information about a target, such as vulnerable web applications, exposed databases, or confidential documents, some examples of predefined search queries include "inurl:/admin/login" to search for login pages within the admin directory of a website, "filetype:sql password" to search for SQL database files containing passwords, and "intitle:index of /etc/passwd" to search for files containing user account information, by using predefined search queries, attackers can quickly identify potential targets for exploitation and gather valuable intelligence about their targets, in addition to these techniques, attackers may also use Google Dorks, which are specialized search queries that are designed to uncover specific types of information about a target, Google Dorks are typically more advanced and targeted than predefined search queries, allowing attackers to uncover highly specific information about their targets, some examples of Google Dorks include "intext:password" to search for web pages containing the word "password", "inurl:/wp-admin" to search for WordPress admin login pages, and "filetype:log inurl:/log" to search for log files containing sensitive information, by using Google Dorks, attackers can uncover valuable information that may be useful in launching targeted cyber attacks or conducting reconnaissance activities, in summary, Google hacking techniques and queries are powerful tools that can be used by both attackers and cybersecurity professionals to uncover sensitive information about a target, by leveraging the advanced search capabilities of Google and combining them with advanced operators, predefined search queries, and Google Dorks, attackers can gather valuable intelligence that may be useful in launching cyber attacks or conducting security assessments.

Chapter 7: Network Scanning: Probing the Target Infrastructure

Network scanning fundamentals are crucial components of cybersecurity operations, enabling organizations to assess the security posture of their networks and identify potential vulnerabilities, network scanning involves systematically scanning network infrastructure to discover hosts, open ports, and services, providing valuable insights into the network's architecture and potential attack vectors, one common tool used for network scanning is Nmap, a powerful open-source tool that allows users to discover hosts and services on a network, Nmap can be deployed using various command-line options, such as "nmap -sP" to perform a ping scan or "nmap -sS" to perform a SYN scan, by specifying different scan types and options, users can customize their scans to meet specific objectives, another tool used for network scanning is Masscan, which is designed for high-speed scanning of large networks, Masscan can be deployed using commands such as "masscan -p1-65535" to scan all ports on a target or "masscan -iL targets.txt" to read target IP addresses from a file, by leveraging Masscan's speed and efficiency, users can quickly identify hosts and open ports on large networks, in addition to these tools, users may also use online services such as Shodan or Censys for network scanning, these services allow users to search for devices and services connected to the internet, providing information such as open ports, banners, and vulnerabilities, by using online services, users can gather intelligence about their network's exposure to the internet and identify potential security risks, in addition to discovering hosts and open ports, network scanning also involves identifying services running on target systems, one common technique for service identification is version detection, which involves determining the version of a service running on a target port, Nmap can perform version detection using the "-sV" option, which sends probes to target ports and analyzes responses to identify service versions, by identifying service versions, users can determine whether services are up-to-date and potentially vulnerable to exploitation, another technique for service identification is banner grabbing, which involves capturing banners or headers returned by servers on target ports, tools like Netcat or Telnet can be used to manually connect to target ports and retrieve banners, by analyzing banners, users can identify specific software versions and configurations, helping them identify potential vulnerabilities, in addition to discovering hosts, open ports, and services, network scanning also involves identifying potential vulnerabilities that may be exploited, one common technique for vulnerability identification is vulnerability scanning, which involves scanning target systems and applications for known vulnerabilities, tools like Nessus or OpenVAS can perform vulnerability scans, generating reports of vulnerabilities based on known signatures and patterns, by identifying vulnerabilities, users can assess their network's security posture and prioritize remediation efforts, in summary, network scanning fundamentals are essential for assessing the security posture of networks and identifying potential vulnerabilities, by leveraging tools such as Nmap, Masscan, and online services like Shodan, users can discover hosts, open ports, and services on their networks, as well as identify potential security risks and prioritize remediation efforts. Types of network scans and their applications encompass a variety of techniques used to assess the security posture of computer networks and identify potential vulnerabilities, one common type of network scan is the ping scan, also known as an ICMP echo request scan, which involves sending ICMP echo requests to target hosts to determine if they are alive, the command "ping target_ip" can be used to perform a ping scan, providing a quick way to identify active hosts on a network, another type of network scan is the TCP SYN scan, which involves sending SYN packets to target ports to determine if they are open, the command "nmap -sS target_ip" can be used to perform a TCP SYN scan, providing information about open ports and potential entry points for exploitation, a related technique is the TCP connect scan, which involves establishing a full TCP connection to target ports to determine if they are open, the command "nmap -sT target_ip" can be used to perform a TCP connect scan, providing similar information to a TCP SYN scan but with a higher chance of detection, yet another type of network scan is the UDP scan, which involves sending UDP packets to target ports to determine if they are open, the command "nmap -sU target_ip" can be used to perform a UDP scan, providing information about open UDP ports and potential vulnerabilities, in addition to these basic types of network scans, there are also more advanced techniques used for specific purposes, such as service version detection, which involves identifying the versions of services running on target ports, the command "nmap -sV target_ip" can be used to perform service version detection, providing information about the software versions and configurations of target services, another advanced technique is OS fingerprinting, which involves identifying the operating systems running on target hosts, the command "nmap -O target_ip" can be used to perform OS fingerprinting, providing information about the operating systems and potential vulnerabilities of target hosts, beyond these standard types of network scans, there are also specialized techniques used for specific applications, such as port scanning, which involves scanning a range of ports on target hosts to identify open ports and potential services, the command "nmap -p1-65535 target_ip" can be used to perform a port scan, providing information about all ports on a target host, another specialized technique is vulnerability scanning, which involves scanning target systems and applications for known vulnerabilities, tools like Nessus or OpenVAS can be used to perform vulnerability scans, generating reports of vulnerabilities based on known signatures and patterns, by identifying vulnerabilities, users can assess their network's security posture and prioritize remediation efforts, in summary, understanding the types of network scans and their applications is essential for assessing the security posture of computer networks and identifying potential vulnerabilities, by leveraging techniques such as ping scans, TCP SYN scans, UDP scans, and advanced techniques like service version detection and OS fingerprinting, users can gather valuable intelligence about their network's exposure to potential threats and prioritize remediation efforts accordingly.

Chapter 8: Enumeration: Extracting Valuable Data

Enumeration process overview is a critical phase in cybersecurity operations, involving the systematic extraction of valuable information from target systems and networks, enumeration provides attackers with insights into the target's resources, users, and configurations, enabling them to identify potential vulnerabilities and plan further exploitation, one common technique used in enumeration is DNS enumeration, which involves querying DNS servers to gather information about a target's domain names, IP addresses, and mail server records, attackers can use tools like 'nslookup' or 'dig' to perform DNS enumeration, issuing commands such as 'nslookup -type=MX domain.com' to retrieve mail server records or 'nslookup -type=NS domain.com' to retrieve name server records, by analyzing DNS information, attackers can gain insights into the target's network topology and potential attack vectors, another technique used in enumeration is SNMP enumeration, which involves querying SNMP-enabled devices to gather information about their configurations and status, attackers can use tools like 'snmpwalk' or 'snmpenum' to perform SNMP enumeration, issuing commands such as 'snmpwalk -c public -v1 target_ip' to retrieve SNMP data from a target device, by analyzing SNMP data, attackers can identify devices, services, and configurations that may be vulnerable to exploitation, yet another technique used in enumeration is LDAP enumeration, which involves querying LDAP servers to gather information about users, groups, and organizational units, attackers can use tools like 'ldapsearch' or 'ldapenum' to perform LDAP enumeration, issuing commands such as 'ldapsearch -x -h target_ip -b "dc=domain,dc=com"' to retrieve LDAP data from a target server, by analyzing LDAP data, attackers can identify users, groups, and permissions that may be exploited in further attacks, in addition to these techniques, attackers may also use SMB enumeration to gather information from Windows-based systems, one common technique is NetBIOS enumeration, which involves querying NetBIOS-enabled devices to gather information about their configurations and shares, attackers can use tools like 'nbtscan' or 'enum4linux' to perform NetBIOS enumeration, issuing commands such as 'nbtscan target_ip' to retrieve NetBIOS data from a target device, by analyzing NetBIOS data, attackers can identify shares, users, and configurations that may be vulnerable to exploitation, in summary, enumeration process overview is a critical phase in cybersecurity operations, enabling attackers to gather valuable information from target systems and networks, by leveraging techniques such as DNS enumeration, SNMP enumeration, LDAP enumeration, and SMB enumeration, attackers can identify potential vulnerabilities and plan further exploitation, understanding the enumeration process and implementing effective security measures is essential for organizations to defend against cyber threats and protect their digital assets from attack. Extracting system and network information through enumeration is a crucial phase in cybersecurity operations, providing attackers with valuable insights into the target's resources, configurations, and potential vulnerabilities, one common technique used in enumeration is DNS enumeration, which involves querying DNS servers to gather information about a target's domain names, IP addresses, and mail server records, attackers can utilize tools like 'nslookup' or 'dig' to perform DNS enumeration, issuing commands such as 'nslookup -type=MX domain.com' to retrieve mail server records or 'nslookup -type=NS domain.com' to retrieve name server records, by analyzing DNS information, attackers can gain insights into the target's network topology and potential attack vectors, another widely used technique in enumeration is SNMP enumeration, which entails querying SNMP-enabled devices to gather information about their configurations and status, attackers can employ tools like 'snmpwalk' or 'snmpenum' to conduct SNMP enumeration, issuing commands such as 'snmpwalk -c public -v1 target_ip' to retrieve SNMP data from a target device, by scrutinizing SNMP data, attackers can identify devices, services, and configurations susceptible to exploitation, yet another prevalent technique in enumeration is LDAP enumeration, which involves querying LDAP servers to gather information about users, groups, and organizational units, attackers can leverage tools like 'ldapsearch' or 'ldapenum' to execute LDAP enumeration, issuing commands such as 'ldapsearch -x -h target_ip -b "dc=domain,dc=com"' to retrieve LDAP data from a target server, by analyzing LDAP data, attackers can uncover users, groups, and permissions vulnerable to exploitation in further attacks, besides these techniques, attackers may also resort to SMB enumeration to extract information from Windows-based systems, a common method is NetBIOS enumeration, which entails querying NetBIOS-enabled devices to gather information about their configurations and shares, attackers can utilize tools like 'nbtscan' or 'enum4linux' to perform NetBIOS enumeration, issuing commands such as 'nbtscan target_ip' to retrieve NetBIOS data from a target device, by scrutinizing NetBIOS data, attackers can identify shares, users, and configurations susceptible to exploitation, in addition to these enumeration techniques, attackers may also employ port scanning to extract system and network information, one common approach is TCP SYN scanning, which involves sending SYN packets to target ports to determine if they are open, attackers can leverage tools like 'nmap' to conduct TCP SYN scans, issuing commands such as 'nmap -sS target_ip' to perform a TCP SYN scan, by analyzing scan results, attackers can identify open ports and potential entry points for exploitation, another approach is UDP scanning, which involves sending UDP packets to target ports to determine if they are open, attackers can use tools like 'nmap' to conduct UDP scans, issuing commands such as 'nmap -sU target_ip' to perform a UDP scan, by scrutinizing scan results, attackers can identify open UDP ports and potential vulnerabilities, overall, extracting system and network information through enumeration is a critical phase in cybersecurity operations, enabling attackers to gather valuable insights into target resources, configurations, and potential vulnerabilities, by leveraging techniques such as DNS enumeration, SNMP enumeration, LDAP enumeration, SMB enumeration, and port scanning, attackers can identify potential vulnerabilities and plan further exploitation, understanding the enumeration process and implementing effective security measures is essential for organizations to defend against cyber threats and protect their digital assets from attack.

Chapter 9: OSINT (Open Source Intelligence) Gathering

Introduction to OSINT, or Open Source Intelligence, is a fundamental aspect of modern intelligence gathering and cybersecurity operations, it involves collecting and analyzing publicly available information from open sources such as the internet, social media, news articles, and government websites, OSINT provides valuable insights into a wide range of topics including individuals, organizations, events, and emerging threats, one common technique used in OSINT is web scraping, which involves automatically extracting information from websites using specialized tools or scripts, attackers can use tools like 'Scrapy' or 'Beautiful Soup' to scrape websites for information such as email addresses, phone numbers, or social media profiles, by analyzing scraped data, attackers can gather intelligence about their targets and identify potential points of entry for exploitation, another technique used in OSINT is social media analysis, which involves monitoring and analyzing social media platforms for information about individuals, organizations, or events, attackers can use tools like 'Maltego' or 'SpiderFoot' to search for social media profiles, track user activity, and identify connections between individuals or groups, by analyzing social media data, attackers can gather insights into their target's behavior, interests, and relationships, helping them craft targeted phishing emails or social engineering attacks, yet another technique used in OSINT is geospatial analysis, which involves analyzing geographic data to identify patterns, trends, or anomalies, attackers can use tools like 'Google Earth' or 'QGIS' to visualize geographic data, such as satellite imagery or GPS coordinates, by analyzing geospatial data, attackers can gather insights into a target's physical locations, infrastructure, or operational activities, helping them plan physical security bypass techniques or conduct reconnaissance activities, in addition to these techniques, OSINT also involves analyzing information from sources such as news articles, government reports, or academic publications, attackers can use tools like 'Google Alerts' or 'RSS feeds' to monitor news sources for information about their targets, by analyzing news articles and reports, attackers can gather intelligence about emerging threats, vulnerabilities, or security incidents, helping them anticipate potential risks and vulnerabilities, in addition to gathering intelligence about potential targets, OSINT can also be used for threat intelligence analysis, which involves monitoring and analyzing open source information to identify emerging threats and trends, organizations can use tools like 'MISP' or 'ThreatConnect' to collect, analyze, and share threat intelligence data with other organizations, by analyzing threat intelligence data, organizations can identify potential threats and vulnerabilities, helping them prioritize security measures and mitigate risks, overall, OSINT is a powerful tool for intelligence gathering and cybersecurity operations, providing valuable insights into a wide range of topics including individuals, organizations, events, and emerging threats, by leveraging techniques such as web scraping, social media analysis, geospatial analysis, and threat intelligence analysis, attackers and organizations can gather intelligence, identify potential risks, and mitigate threats effectively. Leveraging open source tools and platforms for intelligence gathering is a cornerstone of modern cybersecurity and intelligence operations, it involves utilizing a wide range of freely available software and resources to collect, analyze, and disseminate intelligence from open sources, one common category of open source tools used for intelligence gathering is web scraping tools, such as 'Scrapy' or 'Beautiful Soup', which enable users to automatically extract data from websites and web pages, by deploying these tools, analysts can scrape websites for information such as email addresses, phone numbers, or social media profiles, facilitating the collection of valuable intelligence about individuals, organizations, or events, another category of open source tools used for intelligence gathering is social media analysis tools, such as 'Maltego' or 'SpiderFoot', these tools allow users to monitor and analyze social media platforms for information about their targets, by searching for social media profiles, tracking user activity, and identifying connections between individuals or groups, analysts can gather insights into their target's behavior, interests, and relationships, aiding in the identification of potential threats or vulnerabilities, yet another category of open source tools used for intelligence gathering is data visualization tools, such as 'Gephi' or 'Tableau Public', these tools enable users to visualize and analyze large datasets, such as social networks, geospatial data, or financial transactions, by visualizing data in a meaningful way, analysts can identify patterns, trends, or anomalies that may not be apparent from raw data, facilitating the discovery of actionable intelligence, in addition to open source tools, there are also open source platforms and repositories that provide access to a wide range of intelligence gathering resources, one example is the 'OSINT Framework', which is a collection of open source tools, resources, and techniques for intelligence gathering, analysts can use the OSINT Framework to discover new tools, access documentation, and learn about different techniques for gathering intelligence, another example is 'IntelMQ', which is an open source platform for collecting and analyzing threat intelligence data, analysts can use IntelMQ to ingest data from various sources, such as feeds, APIs, or logs, and enrich it with additional context, such as geolocation or threat scores, facilitating the analysis and dissemination of actionable intelligence, moreover, open source platforms like 'MISP' (Malware Information Sharing Platform) enable organizations to share threat intelligence data with other organizations in a standardized format, analysts can use MISP to collaborate with other organizations, share intelligence data, and coordinate responses to emerging threats, by leveraging open source tools and platforms for intelligence gathering, analysts can access a wealth of resources and capabilities to collect, analyze, and disseminate intelligence from open sources effectively, ultimately enhancing their ability to identify and mitigate potential threats and vulnerabilities, furthermore, the open source nature of these tools and platforms promotes transparency, collaboration, and innovation within the cybersecurity and intelligence communities, enabling analysts to stay ahead of emerging threats and adapt to evolving challenges, in summary, leveraging open source tools and platforms for intelligence gathering is essential for modern cybersecurity and intelligence operations, providing analysts with access to a wide range of resources and capabilities to collect, analyze, and disseminate intelligence from open sources effectively, by deploying web scraping tools, social media analysis tools, data visualization tools, and open source platforms like OSINT Framework, IntelMQ, and MISP, analysts can enhance their ability to identify and mitigate potential threats and vulnerabilities, ultimately strengthening their organization's cybersecurity posture.

Chapter 10: Social Media Intelligence Gathering

Social media as a source of intelligence is a critical aspect of modern intelligence gathering and cybersecurity operations, it involves monitoring and analyzing information shared on social media platforms to gather insights into individuals, organizations, events, and emerging threats, one common technique used in social media intelligence gathering is social media scraping, which involves automatically extracting data from social media platforms using specialized tools or scripts, analysts can use tools like 'Scrapy' or 'Twint' to scrape social media platforms for information such as user profiles, posts, comments, and hashtags, by analyzing scraped data, analysts can gain insights into user behavior, interests, and connections, facilitating the identification of potential threats or vulnerabilities, another technique used in social media intelligence gathering is sentiment analysis, which involves analyzing the sentiment or emotion expressed in social media posts or comments, analysts can use tools like 'VADER' or 'TextBlob' to perform sentiment analysis on social media data, categorizing posts or comments as positive, negative, or neutral, by analyzing sentiment data, analysts can identify trends, patterns, or shifts in public opinion, helping them anticipate potential risks or opportunities, yet another technique used in social media intelligence gathering is geolocation analysis, which involves analyzing geographic data associated with social media posts or profiles, analysts can use tools like 'GeoFeedia' or 'Echosec' to search for social media posts based on location or proximity to specific geographic coordinates, by analyzing geolocation data, analysts can identify trends, events, or activities occurring in specific areas, aiding in the identification of potential threats or vulnerabilities, in addition to these techniques, social media intelligence gathering also involves monitoring and analyzing social media trends, topics, or hashtags, analysts can use tools like 'Hashtagify' or 'Trendsmap' to track trending topics or hashtags on social media platforms, by analyzing trending topics, analysts can identify emerging issues, events, or discussions that may be relevant to their organization, helping them anticipate potential risks or opportunities, moreover, social media intelligence gathering also involves monitoring and analyzing social media influencers or key opinion leaders, analysts can use tools like 'Klout' or 'BuzzSumo' to identify influential individuals or organizations on social media platforms, by analyzing influencer data, analysts can identify potential sources of influence or misinformation, helping them assess the credibility or reliability of social media content, furthermore, social media intelligence gathering also involves monitoring and analyzing social media platforms for indicators of potential threats or incidents, analysts can use tools like 'Hootsuite' or 'TweetDeck' to monitor social media platforms for keywords, hashtags, or mentions related to their organization or industry, by analyzing social media data in real-time, analysts can identify potential threats or incidents as they emerge, enabling them to take proactive measures to mitigate risks or respond to incidents, in summary, social media as a source of intelligence is a critical aspect of modern intelligence gathering and cybersecurity operations, providing analysts with valuable insights into individuals, organizations, events, and emerging threats, by leveraging techniques such as social media scraping, sentiment analysis, geolocation analysis, and trend analysis, analysts can gather actionable intelligence from social media platforms, helping them anticipate potential risks or opportunities and protect their organization's interests. Techniques for gathering information from social media platforms are essential components of modern intelligence gathering and cybersecurity operations, they involve a variety of methods and tools to extract valuable insights from the vast amount of data shared on social media, one common technique is social media scraping, which entails automatically extracting data from social media platforms using specialized tools or scripts, analysts can utilize tools like 'Scrapy' or 'Twint' to scrape social media platforms for information such as user profiles, posts, comments, and hashtags, by executing the appropriate commands, analysts can gather large volumes of data that can be further analyzed for intelligence purposes, another technique is sentiment analysis, which involves analyzing the sentiment or emotion expressed in social media posts or comments, analysts can deploy tools like 'VADER' or 'TextBlob' to perform sentiment analysis on social media data, categorizing posts or comments as positive, negative, or neutral, by analyzing sentiment data, analysts can discern public opinion, identify emerging trends, or detect shifts in sentiment that may indicate potential risks or opportunities, yet another technique is geolocation analysis, which involves analyzing geographic data associated with social media posts or profiles, analysts can use tools like 'GeoFeedia' or 'Echosec' to search for social media posts based on location or proximity to specific geographic coordinates, by executing the appropriate commands, analysts can identify trends, events, or activities occurring in specific areas, aiding in the identification of potential threats or vulnerabilities, in addition to these techniques, social media intelligence gathering also involves monitoring and analyzing social media trends, topics, or hashtags, analysts can leverage tools like 'Hashtagify' or 'Trendsmap' to track trending topics or hashtags on social media platforms, by monitoring trending topics, analysts can identify emerging issues, events, or discussions that may be relevant to their organization, facilitating proactive risk management or strategic decision-making, moreover, social media intelligence gathering also encompasses monitoring and analyzing social media influencers or key opinion leaders, analysts can use tools like 'Klout' or 'BuzzSumo' to identify influential individuals or organizations on social media platforms, by analyzing influencer data, analysts can identify potential sources of influence or misinformation, helping them assess the credibility or reliability of social media content, furthermore, social media intelligence gathering involves monitoring and analyzing social media platforms for indicators of potential threats or incidents, analysts can employ tools like 'Hootsuite' or 'TweetDeck' to monitor social media platforms for keywords, hashtags, or mentions related to their organization or industry, by monitoring social media data in real-time, analysts can identify potential threats or incidents as they emerge, enabling them to take timely and effective action to mitigate risks or respond to incidents, overall, techniques for gathering information from social media platforms play a crucial role in intelligence gathering and cybersecurity operations, providing analysts with valuable insights into individuals, organizations, events, and emerging threats, by deploying a combination of techniques such as social media scraping, sentiment analysis, geolocation analysis, trend analysis, and influencer analysis, analysts can gather actionable intelligence from social media platforms, helping them anticipate potential risks or opportunities and protect their organization's interests.

Chapter 11: Tools and Technologies for Reconnaissance

Overview of reconnaissance tools and technologies is crucial for understanding the landscape of information gathering in cybersecurity, it encompasses a wide array of tools and techniques used to gather intelligence about target systems and networks, one of the most fundamental tools in reconnaissance is the 'nmap' command, which is used for network scanning and mapping, analysts can execute commands such as 'nmap -sS target_ip' to perform a TCP SYN scan or 'nmap -sU target_ip' to perform a UDP scan, providing insights into open ports, services, and potential vulnerabilities, another essential tool is 'Maltego', a powerful data visualization tool that allows analysts to map and analyze relationships between entities such as domains, IP addresses, and individuals, by executing commands such as 'maltego', analysts can generate graphical representations of complex data sets, facilitating the identification of patterns, trends, or connections, yet another important tool is 'theHarvester', which is used for email and domain reconnaissance, analysts can deploy commands such as 'theharvester -d domain.com -l 500 -b google' to gather email addresses associated with a target domain from search engines like Google, aiding in the identification of potential targets for phishing attacks or social engineering, in addition to these tools, there are also specialized reconnaissance frameworks like 'Recon-ng', which is a full-featured reconnaissance framework written in Python, analysts can utilize commands such as 'recon-ng' to access a wide range of reconnaissance modules for gathering information from sources like social media, public databases, and DNS records, by executing reconnaissance modules, analysts can gather intelligence about their targets from multiple sources, facilitating comprehensive analysis and decision-making, moreover, there are also specialized tools for reconnaissance in specific domains, such as 'FOCA' for metadata analysis in documents and 'Shodan' for searching for Internet of Things (IoT) devices, by executing commands such as 'foca.exe' or 'shodan search query', analysts can gather intelligence about documents or IoT devices related to their targets, enabling them to identify potential security risks or vulnerabilities, furthermore, there are also open-source intelligence (OSINT) platforms like 'OSINT Framework', which provide access to a wide range of open-source tools and resources for reconnaissance, analysts can use the OSINT Framework to discover new tools, access documentation, and learn about different techniques for gathering intelligence, facilitating comprehensive analysis and decision-making, in summary, an overview of reconnaissance tools and technologies is essential for understanding the landscape of information gathering in cybersecurity, by leveraging tools like 'nmap', 'Maltego', 'theHarvester', and 'Recon-ng', analysts can gather intelligence about their targets from multiple sources, facilitating comprehensive analysis and decision-making, moreover, specialized tools for reconnaissance in specific domains, such as 'FOCA' and 'Shodan', provide analysts with additional capabilities for gathering intelligence, enabling them to identify potential security risks or vulnerabilities, furthermore, open-source intelligence platforms like 'OSINT Framework' provide analysts with access to a wide range of tools and resources for reconnaissance, enhancing their ability to gather intelligence effectively and protect their organization's interests. Evaluating and selecting reconnaissance tools is a critical aspect of cybersecurity operations, it involves assessing the features, capabilities, and suitability of various tools to meet the specific requirements of reconnaissance activities, one important factor to consider when evaluating reconnaissance tools is the type of information that needs to be gathered, different tools specialize in collecting different types of data, for example, tools like 'nmap' are ideal for network scanning and mapping, while tools like 'theHarvester' focus on gathering email addresses and domain information from public sources, analysts can deploy commands such as 'nmap -sS target_ip' or 'theharvester -d domain.com -l 500 -b google' to execute these tools effectively, another factor to consider is the scalability and performance of reconnaissance tools, particularly for large-scale or automated reconnaissance activities, some tools may be better suited for handling large volumes of data or performing tasks in parallel, analysts can assess the scalability of tools by testing them in different scenarios and analyzing their performance metrics, yet another factor to consider is the ease of use and flexibility of reconnaissance tools, particularly for analysts with varying levels of expertise or specialized requirements, some tools may offer intuitive user interfaces, extensive documentation, or support for scripting and automation, enabling analysts to customize and streamline their reconnaissance workflows, analysts can evaluate the ease of use and flexibility of tools by exploring their features, reviewing user feedback, or conducting hands-on testing, in addition to these factors, analysts should also consider the reliability, security, and support of reconnaissance tools, particularly for sensitive or mission-critical reconnaissance activities, some tools may have a proven track record of reliability and security, regular updates, or active community support, analysts can assess the reliability, security, and support of tools by reviewing their development history, security practices, or user forums, in summary, evaluating and selecting reconnaissance tools is a crucial step in cybersecurity operations, by considering factors such as the type of information to be gathered, scalability and performance, ease of use and flexibility, reliability, security, and support, analysts can identify the most suitable tools for their reconnaissance activities, enabling them to gather intelligence effectively and protect their organization's interests.

Chapter 12: Legal and Ethical Considerations in Reconnaissance Activities

Legal frameworks in ethical hacking are essential considerations for cybersecurity professionals and organizations, they provide guidelines, regulations, and laws governing the ethical and legal boundaries of hacking activities, one important legal framework is the Computer Fraud and Abuse Act (CFAA) in the United States, which prohibits unauthorized access to computer systems and networks, analysts must adhere to the provisions of the CFAA to ensure that their hacking activities are conducted within legal boundaries, failure to comply with the CFAA can result in civil and criminal penalties, including fines and imprisonment, another crucial legal framework is the General Data Protection Regulation (GDPR) in the European Union, which regulates the processing and protection of personal data, analysts must ensure that their hacking activities comply with the GDPR to protect the privacy and rights of individuals, violation of the GDPR can result in significant fines and reputational damage for organizations, yet another important legal framework is the Payment Card Industry Data Security Standard (PCI DSS), which governs the security of payment card data, analysts must adhere to the PCI DSS when conducting hacking activities involving payment card data, failure to comply with the PCI DSS can result in fines, penalties, and loss of trust from customers and partners, in addition to these legal frameworks, there are also industry-specific regulations and standards governing ethical hacking activities, such as the Health Insurance Portability and Accountability Act (HIPAA) in the healthcare industry and the Federal Financial Institutions Examination Council (FFIEC) guidelines in the financial services industry, analysts must familiarize themselves with these regulations and standards to ensure compliance with industry-specific requirements, failure to comply with industry-specific regulations can result in legal liabilities and reputational damage for organizations, moreover, ethical hacking activities may also be subject to international laws and treaties governing cybercrime and cybersecurity, such as the Budapest Convention on Cybercrime and the Council of Europe Convention on Data Protection, analysts must consider the implications of international laws and treaties when conducting hacking activities across borders or involving international entities, failure to comply with international laws and treaties can result in legal challenges and diplomatic consequences, furthermore, organizations may also establish internal policies, procedures, and guidelines governing ethical hacking activities, such as acceptable use policies, incident response plans, and rules of engagement for penetration testing, analysts must adhere to these internal policies and guidelines to ensure that their hacking activities align with organizational goals and objectives, failure to comply with internal policies can result in disciplinary action and loss of trust from stakeholders, in summary, legal frameworks in ethical hacking are essential considerations for cybersecurity professionals and organizations, providing guidelines, regulations, and laws governing the ethical and legal boundaries of hacking activities, by adhering to legal frameworks, industry-specific regulations, international laws and treaties, and internal policies and guidelines, analysts can conduct ethical hacking activities responsibly and effectively, protecting the interests and rights of individuals and organizations alike. Ethical guidelines for conducting reconnaissance are fundamental principles that govern the responsible and ethical behavior of cybersecurity professionals during information gathering activities, they provide a framework for ensuring that reconnaissance activities are conducted in a lawful, ethical, and responsible manner, one important ethical guideline is to obtain proper authorization before conducting reconnaissance activities, analysts should ensure that they have explicit permission from the target organization or system owner before initiating any reconnaissance activities, failure to obtain proper authorization can result in legal liabilities and reputational damage for analysts and their organizations, another crucial ethical guideline is to respect the privacy and confidentiality of individuals and organizations during reconnaissance activities, analysts should refrain from collecting or disclosing sensitive information that is not relevant to the purpose of the reconnaissance, such as personal or confidential data, analysts should also avoid intrusive or disruptive reconnaissance techniques that may cause harm or inconvenience to the target organization or its stakeholders, yet another important ethical guideline is to use reconnaissance tools and techniques responsibly and judiciously, analysts should only use tools and techniques that are necessary and appropriate for the reconnaissance objectives, analysts should avoid using reconnaissance tools or techniques that may cause harm or damage to target systems or networks, such as denial-of-service attacks or intrusive scanning techniques, analysts should also avoid using reconnaissance tools or techniques that may violate the terms of service or acceptable use policies of third-party platforms or services, in addition to these ethical guidelines, analysts should also maintain transparency and accountability in their reconnaissance activities, analysts should document and report their reconnaissance activities accurately and responsibly, including the methods, tools, and results of the reconnaissance, analysts should also communicate openly and honestly with stakeholders about the objectives, scope, and outcomes of the reconnaissance, analysts should be prepared to answer questions and address concerns from stakeholders about the legality, ethics, and impact of the reconnaissance activities, moreover, analysts should also continuously evaluate and reassess the ethical implications of their reconnaissance activities, analysts should regularly review and update their ethical guidelines to reflect changes in technology, regulations, and industry standards, analysts should also seek guidance and advice from peers, mentors, or legal experts when uncertain about the ethical implications of specific reconnaissance activities, furthermore, analysts should also consider the potential consequences of their reconnaissance activities on individuals, organizations, and society as a whole, analysts should weigh the risks and benefits of their reconnaissance activities carefully and consider the potential impact on privacy, security, and trust, analysts should strive to minimize harm and maximize positive outcomes in their reconnaissance activities, in summary, ethical guidelines for conducting reconnaissance are essential principles that govern the responsible and ethical behavior of cybersecurity professionals during information gathering activities, by adhering to ethical guidelines, analysts can conduct reconnaissance activities responsibly and ethically, protecting the rights and interests of individuals and organizations alike.

BOOK 2
CERTIFIED ETHICAL HACKER ADVANCED VULNERABILITY ANALYSIS STRATEGIES

ROB BOTWRIGHT

Chapter 1: Introduction to Advanced Vulnerability Analysis

Overview of advanced vulnerability analysis is essential for cybersecurity professionals seeking to identify and mitigate security vulnerabilities in systems and networks, it encompasses a comprehensive examination of software, hardware, and network infrastructure to identify weaknesses that could be exploited by attackers, one important aspect of advanced vulnerability analysis is the use of vulnerability scanning tools, such as 'Nessus' or 'OpenVAS', which automate the process of identifying known vulnerabilities in systems and networks, analysts can deploy these tools to scan target systems and networks for common security issues, such as missing patches, misconfigurations, or insecure settings, by executing the appropriate commands, analysts can initiate vulnerability scans and analyze the results to identify potential security risks, another important aspect of advanced vulnerability analysis is the use of penetration testing techniques, such as 'Metasploit' or 'Burp Suite', which involve actively exploiting vulnerabilities to assess their impact and severity, analysts can deploy these tools to simulate real-world attacks and test the effectiveness of defensive measures, by executing penetration testing modules or scripts, analysts can exploit vulnerabilities in target systems and networks to demonstrate their impact and assess the effectiveness of security controls, yet another important aspect of advanced vulnerability analysis is the use of threat intelligence feeds and databases, which provide information about emerging threats, vulnerabilities, and attack techniques, analysts can leverage threat intelligence feeds to prioritize vulnerabilities based on their likelihood and potential impact, enabling them to focus resources on addressing the most critical security risks, analysts can also use threat intelligence databases to research vulnerabilities and understand their characteristics, enabling them to develop effective mitigation strategies, in addition to these techniques, advanced vulnerability analysis also involves analyzing exploit code and proof-of-concept (PoC) exploits, which demonstrate how vulnerabilities can be exploited in practice, analysts can study exploit code and PoC exploits to understand the underlying vulnerabilities and develop defensive measures, such as intrusion detection signatures or security patches, analysts can also use exploit code and PoC exploits to validate vulnerability findings and assess the risk of exploitation, moreover, advanced vulnerability analysis encompasses the use of specialized techniques, such as fuzzing and reverse engineering, to identify unknown or zero-day vulnerabilities, analysts can deploy fuzzing tools to generate malformed input data and trigger software crashes or unexpected behavior, enabling them to identify potential security vulnerabilities, analysts can also use reverse engineering techniques to analyze software binaries and firmware images for vulnerabilities, such as buffer overflows or logic flaws, enabling them to develop exploits or patches to address these issues, furthermore, advanced vulnerability analysis involves the use of automated vulnerability management platforms, such as 'Qualys' or 'Tenable.io', which provide centralized visibility and control over vulnerability assessment and remediation activities, analysts can use these platforms to automate vulnerability scanning, prioritize remediation efforts, and track progress over time, enabling them to streamline vulnerability management processes and reduce security risks, in summary, an overview of advanced vulnerability analysis is essential for cybersecurity professionals seeking to identify and mitigate security vulnerabilities in systems and networks, by leveraging vulnerability scanning tools, penetration testing techniques, threat intelligence feeds and databases, exploit code and PoC exploits, specialized techniques such as fuzzing and reverse engineering, and automated vulnerability management platforms, analysts can conduct advanced vulnerability analysis effectively, enabling them to proactively identify and address security risks and protect their organization's assets and interests. The importance and scope of advanced vulnerability assessment are paramount in contemporary cybersecurity practices, encompassing a comprehensive examination of systems, networks, and applications to identify security weaknesses that could be exploited by malicious actors, one crucial aspect of advanced vulnerability assessment is its proactive nature, allowing organizations to identify and address security vulnerabilities before they can be exploited, this proactive approach helps organizations reduce the likelihood of security breaches and minimize the potential impact of cyber attacks, another important aspect of advanced vulnerability assessment is its ability to provide organizations with insights into their overall security posture, by identifying and prioritizing vulnerabilities based on their severity and potential impact, organizations can allocate resources more effectively to mitigate the most critical security risks, thereby enhancing their overall security resilience, yet another crucial aspect of advanced vulnerability assessment is its role in compliance and regulatory requirements, many industries and sectors are subject to regulatory mandates that require organizations to conduct regular vulnerability assessments to ensure compliance with security standards and guidelines, failure to comply with these requirements can result in legal liabilities, fines, and reputational damage for organizations, in addition to these factors, the scope of advanced vulnerability assessment extends beyond traditional IT systems and networks to encompass emerging technologies and trends such as cloud computing, internet of things (IoT), and mobile devices, organizations must adapt their vulnerability assessment strategies to address the unique security challenges posed by these technologies, such as dynamic and decentralized infrastructures, diverse attack surfaces, and new threat vectors, moreover, the importance of advanced vulnerability assessment is further underscored by the evolving threat landscape, characterized by increasingly sophisticated cyber attacks and rapidly evolving malware strains, organizations must continuously assess their security posture and adapt their defenses to address emerging threats and vulnerabilities, failure to do so can leave organizations vulnerable to cyber attacks and data breaches, furthermore, advanced vulnerability assessment plays a critical role in supporting incident response and threat intelligence efforts, by regularly assessing and monitoring for vulnerabilities, organizations can detect and respond to security incidents more effectively, enabling them to contain and mitigate the impact of cyber attacks, advanced vulnerability assessment also provides valuable intelligence about emerging threats and attack techniques, helping organizations anticipate and prepare for future security challenges, in summary, the importance and scope of advanced vulnerability assessment are vast and multifaceted, encompassing proactive risk management, compliance and regulatory requirements, emerging technologies and trends, the evolving threat landscape, incident response and threat intelligence, by conducting regular and comprehensive vulnerability assessments, organizations can strengthen their security posture, minimize the risk of cyber attacks, and protect their assets and interests from evolving security threats.

Chapter 2: Exploiting Common Vulnerabilities and Exposures (CVEs)

Understanding Common Vulnerabilities and Exposures (CVEs) and their significance is crucial for cybersecurity professionals and organizations, as CVEs are standardized identifiers for known security vulnerabilities, allowing for easier communication, sharing, and management of vulnerability information, each CVE is assigned a unique identifier number, along with a brief description of the vulnerability, affected software, and potential impact, for example, CVE-2022-1234 may refer to a vulnerability in a specific software application that allows remote code execution, CVEs are maintained and assigned by the MITRE Corporation, which operates the CVE program in collaboration with the global cybersecurity community, the significance of CVEs lies in their role in vulnerability management, organizations can use CVEs to track, prioritize, and remediate known vulnerabilities in their systems and networks, by regularly monitoring CVE databases and advisory sources, organizations can stay informed about emerging threats and vulnerabilities that may impact their security posture, CVEs also play a critical role in vulnerability scanning and assessment tools, such as 'Nessus' or 'OpenVAS', which use CVE identifiers to identify and report known vulnerabilities in systems and networks, analysts can deploy these tools to scan for CVEs and assess their impact on organizational security, facilitating informed decision-making and risk management, another significance of CVEs is their role in security research and collaboration, researchers and security vendors use CVEs to reference and document security vulnerabilities in their findings and advisories, enabling others to replicate and validate their research, share information about vulnerabilities, and develop effective mitigation strategies, CVEs also serve as a common language for communication between security researchers, vendors, and organizations, facilitating collaboration and knowledge sharing across the cybersecurity community, furthermore, CVEs are an important factor in vulnerability disclosure and patch management processes, when a vendor releases a security patch or update to address a CVE, organizations can use the CVE identifier to identify and apply the necessary patches to affected systems, reducing the risk of exploitation and compromise, organizations can also use CVEs to track the status of patches and updates from vendors, ensuring that they are applied in a timely manner to mitigate security risks, in addition to these aspects, understanding CVEs also helps organizations assess the severity and impact of vulnerabilities on their systems and networks, CVEs are assigned severity scores, such as the Common Vulnerability Scoring System (CVSS) score, which provides a standardized method for evaluating the severity of vulnerabilities based on factors such as exploitability, impact, and mitigating factors, organizations can use CVSS scores to prioritize remediation efforts and allocate resources more effectively to address the most critical vulnerabilities, moreover, understanding CVEs also helps organizations assess their exposure to known security risks and make informed decisions about risk acceptance, mitigation, or transfer, by understanding the nature and significance of CVEs, organizations can develop proactive strategies to manage their cybersecurity risks effectively, reducing the likelihood of security breaches and data breaches.

In summary, understanding Common Vulnerabilities and Exposures (CVEs) and their significance is essential for cybersecurity professionals and organizations, as CVEs provide a standardized method for identifying, tracking, and managing known security vulnerabilities, enabling organizations to make informed decisions about risk management, vulnerability remediation, and cybersecurity investments. Techniques for exploiting Common Vulnerabilities and Exposures (CVEs) are essential knowledge for cybersecurity professionals and ethical hackers, as they enable the identification and exploitation of known security vulnerabilities in systems and networks, one common technique for exploiting CVEs is known as "proof-of-concept (PoC) exploit development", which involves creating software code or scripts that demonstrate how a vulnerability can be exploited, for example, security researchers may develop PoC exploits to demonstrate remote code execution or privilege escalation vulnerabilities in software applications, analysts can deploy these PoC exploits to validate the existence and impact of vulnerabilities in target systems, facilitating risk assessment and remediation, another technique for exploiting CVEs is known as "exploit chaining", which involves combining multiple vulnerabilities or attack techniques to achieve a specific objective, such as gaining unauthorized access to a target system or compromising sensitive data, for example, an attacker may chain together a vulnerability in a web application with a misconfigured server to execute a remote code execution attack, analysts can use exploit chaining techniques to simulate real-world attack scenarios and assess the effectiveness of defensive measures, yet another technique for exploiting CVEs is known as "privilege escalation", which involves exploiting vulnerabilities to gain elevated privileges or access rights on a target system, for example, an attacker may exploit a privilege escalation vulnerability in an operating system to gain administrative access and take control of the system, analysts can deploy privilege escalation techniques to assess the security posture of systems and networks and identify potential weaknesses, in addition to these techniques, attackers may also use "exploit kits" or "exploitation frameworks" to automate the process of exploiting CVEs, exploit kits are pre-packaged software tools that contain exploits for known vulnerabilities, while exploitation frameworks provide a platform for developing and executing custom exploits, attackers can deploy exploit kits or exploitation frameworks to launch large-scale attacks against multiple targets, analysts can use these tools to assess the impact of CVEs on organizational security and develop effective mitigation strategies, moreover, attackers may leverage "zero-day exploits" to exploit vulnerabilities that have not yet been publicly disclosed or patched by vendors, zero-day exploits pose a significant threat to organizations as they provide attackers with a window of opportunity to exploit vulnerabilities before they can be remediated, analysts can use threat intelligence feeds and monitoring tools to detect and respond to zero-day exploits in real-time, minimizing the risk of exploitation and compromise, furthermore, attackers may exploit "misconfigurations" or "weaknesses" in systems and networks to achieve their objectives, for example, an attacker may exploit a misconfigured firewall or insecure network service to gain unauthorized access to a target system, analysts can use vulnerability scanning tools and configuration management solutions to identify and remediate misconfigurations and weaknesses in systems and networks, reducing the attack surface and improving security posture, in summary, techniques for exploiting Common Vulnerabilities and Exposures (CVEs) are diverse and evolving, encompassing proof-of-concept exploit development, exploit chaining, privilege escalation, exploit kits, exploitation frameworks, zero-day exploits, misconfigurations, and weaknesses, by understanding these techniques and their implications, cybersecurity professionals can better defend against CVE-based attacks and protect organizational assets and interests from exploitation and compromise.

Chapter 3: Buffer Overflow Exploits and Mitigations

Buffer overflow vulnerabilities are among the most common and dangerous security vulnerabilities found in software applications, they occur when a program writes data beyond the boundaries of a fixed-size buffer in memory, leading to memory corruption and potential exploitation by attackers, one fundamental concept in buffer overflow vulnerabilities is the notion of a buffer, which is a temporary storage area in computer memory used to hold data, buffers have a fixed size, determined by the program's code, and can store a finite amount of data, for example, a buffer may be allocated to hold a string of characters input by a user, another concept in buffer overflow vulnerabilities is the idea of an overflow, which occurs when more data is written to a buffer than it can hold, causing excess data to overflow into adjacent memory locations, this can lead to memory corruption, instability, and unpredictable behavior of the program, yet another concept in buffer overflow vulnerabilities is the distinction between stack-based and heap-based buffer overflows, in a stack-based buffer overflow, the vulnerable buffer is located on the program's call stack, which is used to manage function calls and local variables, attackers exploit stack-based buffer overflows by overwriting return addresses or function pointers stored on the stack, redirecting the program's execution flow to malicious code, in a heap-based buffer overflow, the vulnerable buffer is located in the program's heap, which is used to dynamically allocate memory during program execution, attackers exploit heap-based buffer overflows by corrupting heap metadata or manipulating heap data structures to execute arbitrary code, in addition to these concepts, buffer overflow vulnerabilities can be categorized into several types based on their cause and impact, one common type of buffer overflow is the classic buffer overflow, which occurs when a program fails to properly validate user input before copying it into a buffer, allowing attackers to overwrite critical data and execute arbitrary code, another type of buffer overflow is the stack-based buffer overflow, which occurs when a program writes data beyond the boundaries of a buffer located on the call stack, corrupting stack memory and potentially leading to a stack smashing attack, yet another type of buffer overflow is the heap-based buffer overflow, which occurs when a program writes data beyond the boundaries of a buffer located in the heap, corrupting heap memory and potentially leading to a heap spraying attack, in addition to these types, buffer overflow vulnerabilities can also be classified based on their exploitability and impact, for example, a simple buffer overflow may only result in a program crash or denial of service, while a more sophisticated buffer overflow may allow attackers to gain unauthorized access, escalate privileges, or execute arbitrary code, understanding the concepts and types of buffer overflow vulnerabilities is essential for developers, testers, and security professionals, as it enables them to identify, mitigate, and prevent buffer overflow vulnerabilities in software applications, by implementing secure coding practices, input validation, and memory protection mechanisms, developers can reduce the risk of buffer overflow vulnerabilities and improve the security of their software, similarly, by conducting thorough security testing, including static code analysis and dynamic vulnerability scanning, testers can identify and remediate buffer overflow vulnerabilities before they are exploited by attackers, furthermore, by deploying intrusion detection and prevention systems (IDPS) and applying security patches and updates, security professionals can detect and mitigate buffer overflow attacks in real-time, minimizing the impact on organizational security and integrity, in summary, buffer overflow vulnerabilities pose a significant threat to software security and integrity, understanding the concepts and types of buffer overflow vulnerabilities is essential for effectively identifying, mitigating, and preventing these vulnerabilities in software applications, by implementing secure coding practices, conducting thorough security testing, and deploying appropriate security controls, organizations can reduce the risk of buffer overflow vulnerabilities and enhance the security of their software. Strategies for mitigating buffer overflow exploits are critical for enhancing the security of software applications and protecting against malicious attacks, one fundamental strategy for mitigating buffer overflow exploits is input validation, which involves validating user input to ensure that it conforms to expected formats and ranges, developers can implement input validation by using functions such as 'fgets()' or 'scanf()' in C/C++ to limit the amount of data read into a buffer and prevent buffer overflow vulnerabilities, for example, in a C program, developers can use the 'fgets()' function to read input from the standard input stream and specify the maximum number of characters to read into a buffer, thus preventing buffer overflow vulnerabilities, another strategy for mitigating buffer overflow exploits is bounds checking, which involves checking the size of input data before copying it into a buffer, developers can implement bounds checking by using functions such as 'strncpy()' or 'snprintf()' in C/C++ to ensure that data is copied into a buffer without exceeding its size, for example, in a C program, developers can use the 'strncpy()' function to copy a specified number of characters from one string to another and ensure that the destination buffer is not overflowed, thus preventing buffer overflow vulnerabilities, yet another strategy for mitigating buffer overflow exploits is stack protection, which involves implementing stack canaries or stack cookies to detect and prevent stack-based buffer overflow attacks, developers can enable stack protection mechanisms by using compiler flags such as '-fstack-protector' in GCC or '-stack-protector' in Clang to automatically insert stack canaries into functions that may be vulnerable to buffer overflow attacks, for example, in a C program compiled with GCC, developers can use the '-fstack-protector' flag to enable stack protection and insert stack canaries into vulnerable functions, thus preventing stack-based buffer overflow attacks, in addition to these strategies, developers can also implement address space layout randomization (ASLR) to randomize the memory layout of a process and make it more difficult for attackers to predict the location of code and data, developers can enable ASLR by using compiler flags such as '-pie' or '-fPIE' in GCC to compile position-independent executables (PIE), for example, in a C program compiled with GCC, developers can use the '-pie' flag to compile a PIE executable and enable ASLR, thus increasing the resilience of the application against buffer overflow attacks, moreover, developers can leverage memory-safe programming languages such as Rust or Go to mitigate buffer overflow exploits, these languages provide built-in memory safety features such as bounds checking and automatic memory management, which significantly reduce the risk of buffer overflow vulnerabilities, for example, in a Rust program, developers can use the 'Vec' type to create a resizable array that automatically manages memory allocation and bounds checking, thus preventing buffer overflow vulnerabilities, furthermore, developers can implement runtime exploit mitigation techniques such as stack smashing protection (SSP) or non-executable stack (NX) to detect and prevent buffer overflow exploits at runtime, for example, in a Linux environment, developers can enable SSP and NX by using compiler flags such as '-fstack-protector-strong' and '-Wl,-z,noexecstack' in GCC to compile executables with SSP and NX enabled, thus providing additional layers of defense against buffer overflow attacks, in summary, strategies for mitigating buffer overflow exploits are essential for improving the security of software applications and protecting against malicious attacks, by implementing input validation, bounds checking, stack protection, ASLR, memory-safe programming languages, and runtime exploit mitigation techniques, developers can reduce the risk of buffer overflow vulnerabilities and enhance the resilience of their applications against exploitation.

Chapter 4: Advanced Web Application Vulnerability Assessment

Advanced techniques for assessing web application security are crucial for identifying and mitigating vulnerabilities that could be exploited by attackers, one advanced technique for assessing web application security is penetration testing, which involves simulating real-world attacks on web applications to identify security weaknesses and vulnerabilities, penetration testers, also known as ethical hackers, use a variety of tools and techniques to probe web applications for vulnerabilities, including SQL injection, cross-site scripting (XSS), and remote code execution, for example, testers can use tools such as Burp Suite or OWASP ZAP to intercept and manipulate HTTP requests and responses, enabling them to identify and exploit vulnerabilities in web applications, another advanced technique for assessing web application security is static code analysis, which involves analyzing the source code of web applications to identify potential security vulnerabilities and coding errors, static code analysis tools, such as SonarQube or Checkmarx, scan source code for common security vulnerabilities, such as SQL injection, XSS, and insecure authentication mechanisms, providing developers with actionable insights to remediate vulnerabilities, for example, developers can use SonarQube to analyze Java, C#, or JavaScript code and identify security vulnerabilities, code smells, and other quality issues, enabling them to improve the security and reliability of their web applications, yet another advanced technique for assessing web application security is dynamic application security testing (DAST), which involves testing web applications in a running state to identify security vulnerabilities and weaknesses, DAST tools, such as Acunetix or Netsparker, simulate real-world attacks on web applications by sending malicious input to web forms and endpoints, enabling testers to identify vulnerabilities such as XSS, SQL injection, and insecure file uploads, for example, testers can use Acunetix to scan web applications for vulnerabilities and generate detailed reports with remediation recommendations, enabling developers to patch vulnerabilities and improve the security of their web applications, in addition to these techniques, web application security assessments can also include manual code review, threat modeling, and security architecture review, manual code review involves manually reviewing the source code of web applications to identify security vulnerabilities and coding errors that may have been missed by automated tools, threat modeling involves identifying and prioritizing potential threats and attack vectors against web applications, enabling organizations to allocate resources more effectively to mitigate the most critical security risks, security architecture review involves assessing the design and implementation of security controls in web applications, ensuring that they are aligned with industry best practices and security standards, for example, organizations can use the OWASP Application Security Verification Standard (ASVS) to assess the security posture of their web applications and ensure that they meet security requirements, furthermore, organizations can leverage bug bounty programs and responsible disclosure programs to crowdsource security testing and receive feedback from external security researchers, enabling them to identify and remediate vulnerabilities before they are exploited by attackers, in summary, advanced techniques for assessing web application security are essential for identifying and mitigating vulnerabilities that could be exploited by attackers, by leveraging penetration testing, static code analysis, dynamic application security testing, manual code review, threat modeling, security architecture review, bug bounty programs, and responsible disclosure programs, organizations can improve the security posture of their web applications and protect against cyber threats and attacks. Identification and exploitation of advanced web application vulnerabilities require a comprehensive understanding of web application security principles and techniques, one such vulnerability is SQL injection, which occurs when an attacker injects malicious SQL queries into input fields or parameters of a web application, exploiting vulnerabilities in the underlying database management system, to identify and exploit SQL injection vulnerabilities, attackers can use tools such as SQLMap or manual testing techniques to send crafted SQL queries to the web application and observe the responses, for example, attackers can use SQLMap to automatically detect and exploit SQL injection vulnerabilities in web applications by providing the URL of the target application and specifying the parameters to be tested, another advanced web application vulnerability is cross-site scripting (XSS), which occurs when an attacker injects malicious scripts into web pages viewed by other users, exploiting vulnerabilities in client-side scripts executed by web browsers, to identify and exploit XSS vulnerabilities, attackers can use tools such as XSSer or manual testing techniques to inject malicious scripts into input fields or parameters of the web application and observe the execution of the injected code by other users, for example, attackers can use XSSer to automate the detection and exploitation of XSS vulnerabilities in web applications by providing the URL of the target application and specifying the parameters to be tested, yet another advanced web application vulnerability is remote code execution (RCE), which occurs when an attacker is able to execute arbitrary code on the server hosting the web application, exploiting vulnerabilities in the application's code execution mechanisms, to identify and exploit RCE vulnerabilities, attackers can use tools such as Metasploit or manual testing techniques to send crafted payloads to the web application and execute arbitrary commands on the server, for example, attackers can use Metasploit to exploit RCE vulnerabilities in web applications by selecting a relevant exploit module and providing the necessary parameters, such as the target IP address and port number, in addition to these vulnerabilities, other advanced web application vulnerabilities include XML external entity (XXE) injection, server-side request forgery (SSRF), and insecure deserialization, each of which can be exploited by attackers to achieve various objectives, such as accessing sensitive data, executing arbitrary code, or compromising the integrity of the application, to identify and exploit advanced web application vulnerabilities, organizations can implement a variety of security measures, including secure coding practices, input validation, output encoding, and web application firewalls (WAFs), for example, developers can use frameworks such as OWASP Top 10 or OWASP Cheat Sheet to learn about common web application vulnerabilities and best practices for mitigating them, enabling them to develop more secure applications, organizations can also conduct regular security assessments, such as penetration testing, vulnerability scanning, and code reviews, to identify and remediate vulnerabilities in web applications, for example, organizations can use tools such as Burp Suite or Nessus to scan web applications for vulnerabilities and generate detailed reports with remediation recommendations, enabling developers to patch vulnerabilities and improve the security of their applications, furthermore, organizations can leverage threat intelligence feeds and security incident response teams to monitor for signs of exploitation and respond to attacks in a timely manner, for example, organizations can use tools such as Splunk or Security Information and Event Management (SIEM) systems to aggregate and analyze log data from web servers and detect suspicious activity indicative of a web application attack, in summary, identification and exploitation of advanced web application vulnerabilities require a combination of technical skills, tools, and security measures, by understanding common vulnerabilities and best practices for mitigating them, organizations can improve the security posture of their web applications and protect against cyber threats and attacks.

Chapter 5: Network Protocol Analysis and Exploitation

Network protocol analysis involves the examination and interpretation of network traffic to gain insights into the behavior and characteristics of network protocols, one fundamental concept in network protocol analysis is packet capture, which involves capturing and recording network packets transmitted over a network interface, to capture network packets, analysts can use tools such as Wireshark or tcpdump, for example, to capture packets on the eth0 interface, analysts can use the command 'tcpdump -i eth0 -w capture.pcap', another concept in network protocol analysis is packet inspection, which involves analyzing the contents of captured packets to extract information about the communication between network hosts, to inspect packet contents, analysts can use tools such as Wireshark or tshark, for example, to view the contents of captured packets in

Wireshark, analysts can open the capture file 'capture.pcap' and examine packet details in the packet list pane, yet another concept in network protocol analysis is protocol decoding, which involves interpreting the structure and format of network protocols to understand their behavior and functionality, to decode network protocols, analysts can use tools such as Wireshark or tcpdump, for example, to decode the HTTP protocol in Wireshark, analysts can select an HTTP packet in the packet list pane and view the decoded protocol details in the packet details pane, in addition to these concepts, network protocol analysis also involves traffic analysis, which involves examining patterns and trends in network traffic to identify anomalies and potential security threats, to analyze network traffic, analysts can use tools such as Wireshark or Bro IDS, for example, to analyze HTTP traffic in Wireshark, analysts can apply display filters such as 'http.request.method == "POST"' to filter and analyze POST requests, furthermore, network protocol analysis can also involve flow analysis, which involves tracking the flow of network traffic between hosts and identifying patterns of communication, to perform flow analysis, analysts can use tools such as nfdump or SiLK, for example, to analyze network flows with nfdump, analysts can use the command 'nfdump -r capture.pcap -o extended -s srcip -w flows.txt', in addition to these methods, network protocol analysis can also involve statistical analysis, which involves analyzing network traffic statistics to identify trends and anomalies, to perform statistical analysis, analysts can use tools such as Wireshark or R, for example, to analyze packet capture files with R, analysts can import capture data into R and use statistical functions to calculate metrics such as packet rate, packet size distribution, or protocol distribution, moreover, network protocol analysis can also involve intrusion detection, which involves detecting and responding to malicious activity in network traffic, to perform intrusion detection, analysts can use tools such as Snort or Suricata, for example, to detect HTTP attacks with Snort, analysts can create custom rules to match patterns indicative of malicious activity, such as SQL injection or XSS attacks, finally, network protocol analysis can also involve forensic analysis, which involves reconstructing and analyzing network traffic to investigate security incidents or breaches, to perform forensic analysis, analysts can use tools such as Wireshark or tcpdump, for example, to reconstruct HTTP sessions in Wireshark, analysts can follow TCP streams and examine the contents of HTTP requests and responses, in summary, network protocol analysis is a critical aspect of network security and monitoring, by understanding the concepts and methods of network protocol analysis, analysts can effectively analyze and interpret network traffic to identify security threats, troubleshoot network issues, and investigate security incidents. Exploiting network protocol vulnerabilities for penetration testing is a crucial aspect of assessing the security posture of a network, one commonly exploited network protocol vulnerability is the Address Resolution Protocol (ARP) spoofing attack, which involves spoofing ARP messages to associate an attacker's MAC address with the IP address of a legitimate network host, enabling the attacker to intercept and manipulate network traffic, to perform an ARP spoofing attack, attackers can use tools such as Ettercap or arpspoof, for example, to spoof ARP messages for the IP address 192.168.1.1, attackers can use the command 'arpspoof -i eth0 -t 192.168.1.1', another commonly exploited network protocol vulnerability is the Domain Name System (DNS) cache poisoning attack, which involves injecting malicious DNS records into the cache of a DNS server to redirect users to malicious websites or intercept their traffic, to perform a DNS cache poisoning attack, attackers can use tools such as DNSspoof or Metasploit, for example, to poison the DNS cache of a target DNS server, attackers can use the command 'dnsspoof -i eth0 -f hosts.txt', yet another commonly exploited network protocol vulnerability is the Border Gateway Protocol (BGP) hijacking attack, which involves announcing false routing information to reroute traffic through malicious network paths, enabling attackers to intercept or manipulate network traffic, to perform a BGP hijacking attack, attackers can use tools such as BGPmon or BGPStream, for example, to announce a fake route for the IP prefix 192.168.1.0/24, attackers can use the command 'bgpctl announce 192.168.1.0/24', in addition to these vulnerabilities, other commonly exploited network protocol vulnerabilities include Internet Control Message Protocol (ICMP) redirection, Simple Network Management Protocol (SNMP) enumeration, and Transmission Control Protocol (TCP) session hijacking, each of which can be exploited by attackers to gain unauthorized access to network resources or compromise the integrity and confidentiality of network communications, to exploit network protocol vulnerabilities for penetration testing, ethical hackers or security researchers can use a variety of tools and techniques, including manual testing, automated scanning, and vulnerability exploitation frameworks, for example, ethical hackers can use tools such as Nmap or Nessus to scan for open ports and services on target hosts and identify potential vulnerabilities, once vulnerabilities are identified, ethical hackers can use tools such as Metasploit or ExploitDB to exploit them and gain unauthorized access to target systems, by exploiting network protocol vulnerabilities for penetration testing, organizations can identify and remediate security weaknesses before they are exploited by malicious attackers, thereby improving the overall security posture of their networks, furthermore, organizations can also implement security controls such as network segmentation, access controls, and intrusion detection systems to prevent and detect network protocol vulnerabilities, for example, organizations can use firewalls to restrict access to sensitive network services and prevent unauthorized traffic from entering or leaving the network, overall, exploiting network protocol vulnerabilities for penetration testing is an essential part of assessing and improving the security of networks, by identifying and remedying vulnerabilities, organizations can better protect their assets and data from cyber threats and attacks.

Chapter 6: Advanced Wireless Network Vulnerability Assessment

Challenges and risks in wireless network security are inherent to the nature of wireless communication, one major challenge in wireless network security is the inherent vulnerability of wireless networks to eavesdropping and interception, as wireless signals propagate through the air, they can be intercepted by malicious actors using tools such as Wireshark or Aircrack-ng to capture and analyze network traffic, for example, attackers can use the command 'airodump-ng wlan0' to capture wireless traffic on the wlan0 interface, another challenge in wireless network security is the susceptibility of wireless networks to unauthorized access and intrusion, as wireless networks rely on radio signals to transmit data, they are vulnerable to unauthorized access by attackers who can exploit weaknesses in wireless encryption protocols or authentication mechanisms, for example, attackers can use tools such as Reaver or Wifite to launch brute-force attacks against WPA/WPA2-protected wireless networks, for example, attackers can use the command 'reaver -i wlan0 -b <BSSID> -vv', yet another challenge in wireless network security is the prevalence of rogue access points, which are unauthorized wireless access points deployed within an organization's network infrastructure, rogue access points can be used by attackers to bypass network security controls and gain unauthorized access to sensitive information, for example, attackers can use tools such as Kismet or NetStumbler to detect rogue access points within range of their wireless adapter, for example, attackers can use the command 'kismet -c wlanAdvanced techniques for assessing and securing wireless networks are essential in the ever-evolving landscape of cybersecurity, one such technique is wireless penetration testing, which involves simulating attacks against wireless networks to identify vulnerabilities and weaknesses, to conduct wireless penetration testing, security professionals can use tools such as Aircrack-ng or Wifite to capture and analyze wireless traffic, for example, they can use the command 'airmon-ng start wlan0' to put their wireless adapter into monitor mode and 'airodump-ng wlan0mon' to capture wireless traffic, another advanced technique for assessing and securing wireless networks is rogue access point detection, which involves identifying unauthorized wireless access points within an organization's network infrastructure, to detect rogue access points, security professionals can use tools such as NetStumbler or Kismet to scan for wireless networks and identify devices with suspicious or unknown SSIDs, for example, they can use the command 'kismet -c wlan0' to start scanning for wireless networks, yet another advanced technique for assessing and securing wireless networks is wireless intrusion detection and prevention systems (WIDPS), which monitor wireless traffic for suspicious activity and automatically respond to potential threats, to deploy a WIDPS, organizations can use tools such as Snort or Suricata configured with wireless intrusion detection rules, for example, they can use the command 'snort -dev -c /etc/snort/snort.conf' to start Snort in detection mode, in addition to these techniques, other advanced methods for assessing and securing wireless networks include spectrum analysis, which involves analyzing the frequency spectrum to identify sources of interference or unauthorized wireless signals, to perform spectrum analysis, organizations can use tools such as Wi-Spy or Kismet with a compatible spectrum analyzer, for example, they can use the command 'kismet -c wlan0 --spectimeout 20' to start spectrum analysis, furthermore, advanced encryption techniques such as Wi-Fi Protected Access 3 (WPA3) and Enterprise WPA2 with 802.1X authentication can enhance the security of wireless networks by providing stronger encryption and authentication mechanisms, organizations can deploy WPA3 or Enterprise WPA2 with 802.1X authentication using tools such as FreeRADIUS or Cisco Identity Services Engine (ISE) for centralized authentication and access control, for example, they can use the command 'apt-get install freeradius' to install FreeRADIUS on a Linux system, moreover, implementing wireless intrusion prevention systems (WIPS) can help organizations proactively identify and mitigate wireless threats by automatically blocking unauthorized devices or rogue access points, organizations can deploy WIPS solutions such as Cisco Meraki Wireless Intrusion Prevention or Aruba Wireless Intrusion Detection and Prevention, for example, they can use the command 'apt-get install aruba-wips' to install Aruba WIPS on a Linux system, in summary, advanced techniques for assessing and securing wireless networks are critical for protecting sensitive information and maintaining the integrity and confidentiality of wireless communications, by leveraging advanced tools and technologies, organizations can effectively identify and mitigate security risks in their wireless environments, thereby enhancing overall network security posture and reducing the likelihood of successful cyber attacks.

Chapter 7: Exploiting Privilege Escalation Vulnerabilities

Understanding privilege escalation vulnerabilities is crucial in the field of cybersecurity as they represent a significant threat to the security of computer systems and networks, one common type of privilege escalation vulnerability is known as local privilege escalation, which occurs when a low-privileged user gains unauthorized access to higher privileges on a system, typically, attackers exploit local privilege escalation vulnerabilities to escalate their privileges from a standard user to an administrator or root user, enabling them to perform malicious actions such as installing malware, stealing sensitive data, or modifying system configurations, to identify local privilege escalation vulnerabilities, security professionals can use tools such as Windows Exploit Suggester or Linux Exploit Suggester to search for known vulnerabilities in the target operating system, for example, they can use the command 'windows-exploit-suggester.py --update' to update the exploit database and 'windows-exploit-suggester.py --systeminfo systeminfo.txt' to analyze the system information and suggest potential exploits, another type of privilege escalation vulnerability is remote privilege escalation, which occurs when an attacker gains unauthorized access to higher privileges on a remote system, typically, attackers exploit remote privilege escalation vulnerabilities by exploiting vulnerabilities in network services or protocols, such as buffer overflows, command injection, or authentication bypasses, to identify remote privilege escalation vulnerabilities, security professionals can use tools such as Nessus or OpenVAS to scan for vulnerabilities in network services and applications, for example, they can use the command 'nessuscli scan --targets 192.168.1.0/24' to perform a network vulnerability scan and identify potential remote privilege escalation vulnerabilities, in addition to local and remote privilege escalation vulnerabilities, other types of privilege escalation vulnerabilities include vertical privilege escalation, which occurs when a user gains unauthorized access to higher privileges within the same user role, and horizontal privilege escalation, which occurs when a user gains unauthorized access to privileges belonging to another user or role, to mitigate privilege escalation vulnerabilities, organizations can implement security best practices such as least privilege principle, which involves restricting user privileges to the minimum level necessary to perform their tasks, and privilege separation, which involves separating privileged and non-privileged operations to reduce the impact of privilege escalation attacks, for example, organizations can use the command 'sudo' to restrict user privileges on Unix-based systems, and 'icacls' to manage file and folder permissions on Windows systems, furthermore, organizations can also deploy security controls such as intrusion detection systems, endpoint security solutions, and access control mechanisms to detect and prevent privilege escalation attacks, for example, organizations can use tools such as Snort or Suricata to monitor network traffic for signs of privilege escalation attempts and 'AppLocker' or 'Windows Defender Application Control' to restrict the execution of unauthorized applications on Windows systems, overall, understanding privilege escalation vulnerabilities is essential for effective cybersecurity, by identifying and mitigating these vulnerabilities, organizations can enhance the security of their systems and networks and reduce the risk of unauthorized access and data breaches. Techniques for exploiting and mitigating privilege escalation are essential components of cybersecurity strategy, one common technique for exploiting privilege escalation vulnerabilities is through the use of misconfigured file permissions, attackers can exploit weak file permissions to gain elevated privileges and execute malicious commands, for example, they can use the 'chmod' command to modify file permissions and grant themselves additional privileges, another technique for exploiting privilege escalation vulnerabilities is through the exploitation of software vulnerabilities, attackers can exploit vulnerabilities in operating systems or applications to gain unauthorized access to higher privileges, for example, they can use the 'msfconsole' command to launch Metasploit and search for exploits targeting specific software vulnerabilities, in addition to these techniques, attackers can also exploit weak authentication mechanisms to escalate their privileges, for example, they can use default or weak credentials to gain unauthorized access to administrative accounts and escalate their privileges, for example, they can use the 'ssh' command to connect to a remote system using a specified username and password, furthermore, attackers can exploit misconfigured access control lists (ACLs) to escalate their privileges, for example, they can use the 'icacls' command on Windows systems to view and modify file and folder permissions, to mitigate privilege escalation vulnerabilities, organizations can implement security best practices such as least privilege principle, which involves restricting user privileges to the minimum level necessary to perform their tasks, for example, they can use the 'sudo' command on Unix-based systems to restrict user privileges, another technique for mitigating privilege escalation vulnerabilities is through the use of access control mechanisms such as role-based access control (RBAC), organizations can use RBAC to define and enforce access control policies based on user roles and responsibilities, for example, they can use the 'setfacl' command on Linux systems to set access control lists (ACLs) based on user roles, in addition to these techniques, organizations can also implement intrusion detection systems (IDS) and intrusion prevention systems (IPS) to detect and prevent privilege escalation attacks, for example, they can use tools such as Snort or Suricata to monitor network traffic for signs of privilege escalation attempts, and 'AppLocker' or 'Windows Defender Application Control' to restrict the execution of unauthorized applications on Windows systems, furthermore, organizations can also conduct regular security audits and vulnerability assessments to identify and remediate privilege escalation vulnerabilities, for example, they can use tools such as Nessus or OpenVAS to scan for vulnerabilities in network services and applications, and 'lynis' or 'chkrootkit' to perform system integrity checks and detect signs of compromise, overall, techniques for exploiting and mitigating privilege escalation vulnerabilities are critical for ensuring the security of computer systems and networks, by understanding and implementing these techniques, organizations can reduce the risk of unauthorized access and data breaches.

Chapter 8: Reverse Engineering and Malware Analysis

Reverse engineering and malware analysis are integral components of cybersecurity, allowing analysts to understand the inner workings of malicious software and develop countermeasures to protect against cyber threats, reverse engineering involves the process of analyzing a software program or system to understand its functionality, structure, and behavior, one common technique used in reverse engineering is disassembly, which involves converting machine code into assembly language to understand the instructions executed by the program, analysts can use tools such as IDA Pro or Ghidra to disassemble binary executables and analyze their code, for example, they can use the 'ida' command to launch IDA Pro and load a binary executable for analysis, another technique used in reverse engineering is decompilation, which involves converting machine code or assembly language into a higher-level programming language, such as C or C++, to facilitate analysis and understanding, analysts can use tools such as RetDec or Hex-Rays Decompiler to decompile binary executables into source code, for example, they can use the 'retdec-decompiler' command to decompile a binary executable into C code, in addition to these techniques, analysts can also use dynamic analysis techniques to understand the behavior of a program at runtime, dynamic analysis involves executing the program in a controlled environment and monitoring its behavior, such as system calls, network traffic, and file operations, analysts can use tools such as Wireshark or Process Monitor to capture and analyze system activity during program execution, for example, they can use the 'wireshark' command to launch Wireshark and capture network traffic generated by a program, malware analysis is a specialized form of reverse engineering focused on analyzing malicious software, such as viruses, worms, and trojans, to understand how they operate and develop countermeasures to protect against them, one common technique used in malware analysis is static analysis, which involves analyzing the binary code or file structure of a malware sample without executing it, analysts can use tools such as PEiD or FileInsight to analyze the structure and characteristics of a malware sample, for example, they can use the 'peid' command to launch PEiD and scan a malware sample for known characteristics, another technique used in malware analysis is dynamic analysis, which involves executing the malware sample in a controlled environment, such as a sandbox or virtual machine, and monitoring its behavior, analysts can use tools such as Cuckoo Sandbox or VMRay Analyzer to automate the dynamic analysis process and capture information about the malware's behavior, for example, they can use the 'cuckoo' command to launch Cuckoo Sandbox and analyze a malware sample in a virtual environment, in addition to these techniques, analysts can also use code analysis techniques to understand the functionality and logic of a malware sample, code analysis involves analyzing the instructions and logic flow of a malware sample to identify its capabilities and behavior, analysts can use tools such as IDA Pro or OllyDbg to disassemble and debug a malware sample, for example, they can use the 'ollydbg' command to launch OllyDbg and debug a malware sample, overall, reverse engineering and malware analysis are essential skills for cybersecurity professionals, enabling them to understand the tactics, techniques, and procedures used by attackers and develop effective strategies to defend against cyber threats. Tools and techniques for analyzing malicious code are essential components of cybersecurity, enabling analysts to understand the behavior and functionality of malicious software and develop effective countermeasures to protect against cyber threats, one common tool used for analyzing malicious code is disassemblers, which allow analysts to convert machine code into assembly language for manual analysis, popular disassemblers include IDA Pro and Ghidra, analysts can use these tools to disassemble binary executables and examine the assembly instructions to understand how the malware operates, for example, they can use the 'ida' command to launch IDA Pro and load a malware sample for analysis, another tool used for analyzing malicious code is debuggers, which allow analysts to execute malware samples in a controlled environment and monitor their behavior, popular debuggers include OllyDbg and WinDbg, analysts can use these tools to set breakpoints, inspect memory, and step through the code to identify malicious behavior, for example, they can use the 'ollydbg' command to launch OllyDbg and debug a malware sample, in addition to disassemblers and debuggers, analysts also use static analysis tools to examine the structure and characteristics of malware samples without executing them, popular static analysis tools include PEiD and FileInsight, analysts can use these tools to analyze file headers, import/export tables, and embedded resources to identify indicators of compromise, for example, they can use the 'peid' command to launch PEiD and scan a malware sample for known characteristics, dynamic analysis tools are also widely used for analyzing malicious code, these tools allow analysts to execute malware samples in a controlled environment and monitor their behavior in real-time, popular dynamic analysis tools include Cuckoo Sandbox and VMRay Analyzer, analysts can use these tools to capture system calls, network traffic, and file operations to understand the malware's behavior, for example, they can use the 'cuckoo' command to launch Cuckoo Sandbox and analyze a malware sample in a virtual environment, furthermore, analysts also use code analysis techniques to examine the functionality and logic of malicious code, this involves analyzing the instructions and control flow of the malware to identify its capabilities and behavior, tools such as IDA Pro and Radare2 are commonly used for code analysis, analysts can use these tools to disassemble, decompile, and debug the malware code, for example, they can use the 'radare2' command to launch Radare2 and analyze a malware sample, overall, tools and techniques for analyzing malicious code are critical for cybersecurity professionals, enabling them to understand the tactics, techniques, and procedures used by attackers and develop effective strategies to defend against cyber threats.

Chapter 9: Exploiting Cryptographic Weaknesses

Identifying and exploiting cryptographic weaknesses is a fundamental aspect of cybersecurity, as cryptographic algorithms are commonly used to secure sensitive data and communications, one common cryptographic weakness is the use of weak or outdated algorithms, such as the Data Encryption Standard (DES) or the Rivest Cipher (RC4), which are vulnerable to brute-force attacks and other cryptographic attacks, to identify cryptographic weaknesses, security professionals can use tools such as OpenSSL or Nmap to scan for vulnerable cryptographic algorithms and configurations, for example, they can use the 'openssl' command to test for weak SSL/TLS cipher suites on a web server, another cryptographic weakness is the improper implementation of cryptographic algorithms, such as using insecure random number generators or insecure key management practices, which can lead to vulnerabilities such as key reuse or key leakage, to exploit these weaknesses, attackers can use tools such as John the Ripper or Hashcat to crack weak cryptographic keys or passwords, for example, they can use the 'john' command to crack password hashes using a dictionary attack, in addition to these techniques, attackers can also exploit cryptographic weaknesses through side-channel attacks, which involve monitoring the physical characteristics of a cryptographic device, such as power consumption or electromagnetic radiation, to extract cryptographic keys or sensitive information, to mitigate cryptographic weaknesses, organizations can implement security best practices such as using strong cryptographic algorithms and key lengths, regularly updating cryptographic libraries and configurations, and implementing cryptographic protocols and standards, for example, they can use the 'ssh-keygen' command to generate strong SSH keys with a minimum length of 2048 bits, furthermore, organizations can also deploy cryptographic hardware security modules (HSMs) to securely generate, store, and manage cryptographic keys, for example, they can use the 'openssl genpkey' command to generate a new private key and store it securely in an HSM, overall, identifying and exploiting cryptographic weaknesses is essential for cybersecurity professionals to understand, as it allows them to assess the security of cryptographic systems and develop effective strategies to defend against cryptographic attacks and protect sensitive information. Mitigating cryptographic vulnerabilities is a crucial aspect of cybersecurity strategy, as cryptographic techniques are integral for securing data and communications in modern computing environments, one common cryptographic vulnerability is the use of weak cryptographic algorithms or key lengths, which can be susceptible to attacks such as brute force or cryptanalysis, to mitigate this vulnerability, organizations should ensure that they use strong cryptographic algorithms and key lengths recommended by cryptographic standards bodies such as the National Institute of Standards and Technology (NIST) or the International Organization for Standardization (ISO), for example, they can use the 'openssl genrsa' command to generate RSA keys with a minimum length of 2048 bits, another cryptographic vulnerability is the improper implementation of cryptographic protocols or algorithms, which can lead to vulnerabilities such as padding oracle attacks or protocol downgrade attacks, to mitigate this vulnerability, organizations should regularly update their cryptographic libraries and configurations to patch known vulnerabilities and ensure that they follow best practices for implementing cryptographic protocols, for example, they can use the 'apt-get update' command to update the OpenSSL library on a Debian-based Linux system, in addition to these techniques, organizations should also implement strong key management practices to protect cryptographic keys from unauthorized access or disclosure, this includes using secure key storage mechanisms such as hardware security modules (HSMs) or key management services (KMS), and regularly rotating cryptographic keys to limit the impact of key compromise, for example, they can use the 'aws kms create-key' command to create a new encryption key in AWS Key Management Service (KMS), furthermore, organizations should also implement cryptographic protections for data in transit and data at rest, this includes using strong encryption algorithms and protocols to encrypt sensitive data before transmitting it over a network or storing it on disk, and using secure communication channels such as TLS/SSL for transmitting sensitive data over the internet, for example, they can use the 'openssl enc' command to encrypt a file using AES encryption, overall, mitigating cryptographic vulnerabilities requires a multi-faceted approach that includes using strong cryptographic algorithms and protocols, implementing secure key management practices, and regularly updating cryptographic libraries and configurations to patch known vulnerabilities.

Chapter 10: Fuzzing Techniques for Vulnerability Discovery

Fuzzing, also known as fuzz testing or fuzzing, is a software testing technique used to discover vulnerabilities in software applications by providing invalid, unexpected, or random data as inputs and monitoring the application's behavior for unexpected crashes or errors, the primary goal of fuzzing is to identify and fix security vulnerabilities, memory leaks, and other software bugs before they can be exploited by attackers, fuzzing is particularly important in the field of cybersecurity, as software vulnerabilities are often exploited by attackers to gain unauthorized access to systems, steal sensitive data, or disrupt services, one of the key advantages of fuzzing is its ability to uncover unknown vulnerabilities that may not be detected by traditional testing techniques such as manual code review or automated static analysis, to perform fuzz testing, security professionals can use various fuzzing tools and frameworks such as American Fuzzy Lop (AFL), Peach Fuzzer, or libFuzzer, these tools generate and execute a large number of test cases with invalid or unexpected inputs to identify vulnerabilities in the target software, for example, they can use the 'afl-fuzz' command to launch AFL and fuzz a target binary executable, fuzzing can be applied to a wide range of software components, including web applications, network protocols, file formats, and APIs, by fuzzing these components, security professionals can identify vulnerabilities such as buffer overflows, format string vulnerabilities, integer overflows, and memory corruption bugs, which can be exploited by attackers to compromise the security of a system, in addition to uncovering vulnerabilities, fuzzing can also be used to assess the resilience of software applications to unexpected inputs and error conditions, by subjecting an application to a wide range of inputs and monitoring its behavior, security professionals can evaluate how the application handles unexpected situations and identify areas for improvement, for example, they can use the 'peach' command to launch Peach Fuzzer and fuzz a target web application, overall, fuzzing is a critical component of the software development lifecycle and a valuable technique for improving the security and reliability of software applications, by systematically testing applications with invalid or unexpected inputs, security professionals can identify and fix vulnerabilities before they can be exploited by attackers, thereby reducing the risk of security breaches and protecting sensitive data. Fuzzing techniques and strategies play a pivotal role in vulnerability discovery and software testing, offering a systematic approach to uncovering security flaws and weaknesses in software applications, one of the primary fuzzing techniques is mutation-based fuzzing, which involves modifying existing valid inputs to create malformed or invalid test cases, these mutated inputs are then fed into the target application to trigger unexpected behavior and potential vulnerabilities, security professionals can use mutation-based fuzzing tools such as AFL or libFuzzer to automatically generate and execute mutated test cases, for example, they can use the 'afl-cmin' command to minimize a set of input files for efficient fuzzing with AFL, another fuzzing technique is generation-based fuzzing, which involves generating entirely new test cases from scratch using predefined templates or grammars, these generated test cases are designed to cover a wide range of inputs and edge cases, allowing security professionals to explore different paths and scenarios in the target application, security professionals can use generation-based fuzzing tools such as Peach Fuzzer or SPIKE to create and execute custom test cases, for example, they can use the 'spike' command to generate custom test cases with SPIKE, in addition to these techniques, hybrid fuzzing combines mutation-based and generation-based fuzzing approaches to leverage their respective strengths, this hybrid approach allows security professionals to efficiently explore the input space of the target application while maximizing code coverage and vulnerability discovery, security professionals can use hybrid fuzzing tools such as AFLSmart or AFLFast to combine mutation-based and generation-based fuzzing, for example, they can use the 'afl-smart' command to perform hybrid fuzzing with AFLSmart, furthermore, directed fuzzing is another important strategy for maximizing the effectiveness of fuzzing, this approach involves guiding the fuzzing process towards specific code paths or functionalities in the target application that are likely to contain vulnerabilities, security professionals can use techniques such as code coverage analysis, symbolic execution, or taint analysis to identify interesting code paths and guide the fuzzing process accordingly, for example, they can use the 'afl-cov' command to perform code coverage analysis with AFL, overall, fuzzing techniques and strategies are essential for effective vulnerability discovery and software testing, by systematically generating and executing malformed or invalid inputs, security professionals can uncover hidden vulnerabilities and weaknesses in software applications, enabling developers to fix these issues before they can be exploited by attackers, thereby enhancing the security and reliability of software systems.

Chapter 11: Vulnerability Management and Patch Management Strategies

Effective vulnerability management strategies are integral components of robust cybersecurity frameworks, offering systematic approaches to identify, assess, prioritize, and mitigate security vulnerabilities across an organization's IT infrastructure, one key aspect of effective vulnerability management is vulnerability scanning, which involves using automated tools to scan networks, systems, and applications for known vulnerabilities and misconfigurations, organizations can use vulnerability scanning tools such as Nessus, OpenVAS, or Qualys to perform regular vulnerability scans, for example, they can use the 'nessus' command to launch Nessus and scan a target network for vulnerabilities, another important aspect of vulnerability management is vulnerability assessment, which involves analyzing the impact and severity of identified vulnerabilities to prioritize remediation efforts, security professionals can use vulnerability assessment tools such as the Common Vulnerability Scoring System (CVSS) to assess the severity of vulnerabilities based on factors such as exploitability and impact, for example, they can use the 'cvss' command to calculate the CVSS score for a given vulnerability, in addition to vulnerability scanning and assessment, organizations should also establish robust patch management processes to promptly address known vulnerabilities and apply security patches to vulnerable systems and software, this includes regularly monitoring vendor security advisories and software update notifications to identify and deploy relevant patches in a timely manner, for example, they can use the 'yum update' command to update packages on a CentOS-based Linux system, furthermore, organizations should implement vulnerability remediation strategies that prioritize high-risk vulnerabilities with the greatest potential impact on the organization's security posture, this involves establishing risk-based prioritization criteria to allocate resources and prioritize remediation efforts effectively, for example, they can use risk scoring models such as the Common Vulnerability Risk Analysis Framework (CVRAF) to prioritize vulnerabilities based on their potential impact on critical assets or business processes, moreover, vulnerability management should be an ongoing and iterative process that involves continuous monitoring, analysis, and improvement, organizations should regularly review and update their vulnerability management processes and procedures to adapt to evolving threats and technologies, for example, they can use the 'vuln' command to generate vulnerability reports and track remediation progress, overall, effective vulnerability management requires a comprehensive and proactive approach that involves vulnerability scanning, assessment, patch management, remediation, and continuous improvement, by implementing robust vulnerability management strategies, organizations can enhance their security posture, mitigate risks, and protect against cyber threats effectively. Best practices for patch management in cybersecurity are essential for maintaining the security and integrity of an organization's IT infrastructure, patch management involves the process of identifying, deploying, and managing software updates or patches to address security vulnerabilities and software bugs, one fundamental aspect of patch management is to establish a comprehensive inventory of all software and hardware assets within the organization's IT environment, this includes maintaining an up-to-date inventory of operating systems, applications, devices, and firmware versions deployed across the network, organizations can use asset management tools such as Snipe-IT or

Lansweeper to create and maintain an inventory of IT assets, for example, they can use the 'snipeit' command to launch the Snipe-IT web interface and manage IT assets, once the inventory is established, organizations should regularly monitor vendor security advisories, vulnerability databases, and software update notifications to identify and prioritize relevant patches for deployment, this includes subscribing to security mailing lists, following vendor blogs, and monitoring industry news for information about newly discovered vulnerabilities and available patches, for example, they can use the 'nvd' command to search the National Vulnerability Database (NVD) for information about known vulnerabilities, moreover, organizations should establish patch deployment processes and procedures to ensure timely and consistent patching across the IT environment, this includes defining patch deployment schedules, roles and responsibilities, testing procedures, and rollback plans, organizations can use patch management tools such as WSUS (Windows Server Update Services), SCCM (System Center Configuration Manager), or Ansible to automate patch deployment and streamline the patching process, for example, they can use the 'wsusutil' command to manage WSUS on a Windows Server, furthermore, organizations should prioritize patches based on risk and criticality to focus resources on addressing high-risk vulnerabilities that pose the greatest threat to the organization's security posture, this involves establishing risk-based prioritization criteria that take into account factors such as the severity of the vulnerability, exploitability, and potential impact on business operations, organizations can use vulnerability scoring models such as CVSS (Common Vulnerability Scoring System) to assess the severity of vulnerabilities and prioritize patches accordingly, for example, they can use the 'cvss' command to calculate the CVSS score for a given vulnerability, additionally, organizations should implement a robust testing process to validate patches before deployment to minimize the risk of unintended consequences or system disruptions, this includes testing patches in a controlled environment that mirrors the production environment to identify any compatibility issues, conflicts, or regressions, organizations can use testing tools such as Docker or VirtualBox to create isolated testing environments for patch validation, for example, they can use the 'docker' command to create a Docker container for testing patches, overall, effective patch management requires a proactive and systematic approach that includes inventory management, vulnerability monitoring, patch deployment, prioritization, testing, and continuous improvement, by implementing best practices for patch management, organizations can reduce their exposure to security risks, improve their overall security posture, and protect against cyber threats effectively.

Chapter 12: Ethical Hacking Methodologies for Vulnerability Analysis

Ethical hacking methodologies and frameworks provide structured approaches to conducting ethical hacking activities and penetration testing engagements, one of the most widely used ethical hacking frameworks is the Penetration Testing Execution Standard (PTES), which outlines a comprehensive methodology for planning, executing, and reporting penetration tests, PTES defines several distinct phases of a penetration test, including pre-engagement, intelligence gathering, threat modeling, vulnerability analysis, exploitation, post-exploitation, and reporting, organizations can use PTES as a guide to conduct systematic and thorough penetration tests that identify security weaknesses and vulnerabilities in their IT infrastructure, for example, they can use the 'ptes' command to access the PTES documentation and resources, another popular ethical hacking methodology is the Open Source Security Testing Methodology Manual (OSSTMM), which provides a structured approach to security testing that focuses on real-world scenarios and business risks, OSSTMM covers a wide range of security testing activities, including vulnerability assessment, penetration testing, security auditing, and risk analysis, organizations can use OSSTMM to assess the security posture of their systems and applications and identify areas for improvement, for example, they can use the 'osstmm' command to download the OSSTMM documentation and tools, moreover, the Information Systems Security Assessment Framework (ISSAF) is another ethical hacking framework that provides guidance on conducting security assessments and penetration tests, ISSAF offers a structured approach to information security assessments that covers all aspects of the assessment process, including planning, execution, and reporting, organizations can use ISSAF to assess the effectiveness of their security controls and identify weaknesses in their defenses, for example, they can use the 'issaf' command to access the ISSAF documentation and templates, additionally, the National Institute of Standards and Technology (NIST) has developed the NIST Special Publication 800-115, which provides guidance on conducting information security assessments and penetration tests, NIST SP 800-115 outlines a systematic approach to assessing and testing the security controls of an organization's IT systems and applications, organizations can use NIST SP 800-115 to ensure that their security assessments are conducted in a thorough and consistent manner, for example, they can use the 'nist' command to access the NIST SP 800-115 publication and related resources, furthermore, the Cyber Kill Chain is a popular framework developed by Lockheed Martin that describes the stages of a cyber attack from the perspective of an adversary, the Cyber Kill Chain consists of seven stages: reconnaissance, weaponization, delivery, exploitation, installation, command and control, and actions on objectives, organizations can use the Cyber Kill Chain framework to understand how cyber attacks are conducted and develop defensive strategies to detect, prevent, and respond to attacks, for example, they can use the 'cyberkillchain' command to access the Cyber Kill Chain documentation and resources, overall, ethical hacking methodologies and frameworks provide valuable guidance and structure for conducting security assessments and penetration tests, by following established methodologies and frameworks, organizations can identify and address security vulnerabilities effectively, mitigate risks, and improve their overall security posture. Integrating ethical hacking into vulnerability analysis processes is crucial for enhancing the effectiveness and comprehensiveness of security assessments, one method of integration is to incorporate ethical hacking techniques and methodologies into existing vulnerability assessment frameworks, such as the Penetration Testing Execution Standard (PTES) or the Open Source Security Testing Methodology Manual (OSSTMM), organizations can use these frameworks as guidelines for conducting systematic and thorough security assessments that leverage ethical hacking techniques to identify vulnerabilities and security weaknesses, for example, they can use the 'ptes' command to access the PTES documentation and resources, another approach to integrating ethical hacking into vulnerability analysis processes is to establish dedicated ethical hacking teams or roles within the organization, these teams are responsible for conducting ethical hacking activities, such as penetration testing, red team exercises, and vulnerability research, organizations can leverage these teams to proactively identify and exploit security vulnerabilities before malicious actors do, for example, they can use the 'redteam' command to establish a dedicated red team within the organization, moreover, organizations can integrate ethical hacking into their vulnerability management processes by using ethical hacking techniques to validate and verify the effectiveness of security controls and patches, for example, they can use penetration testing to assess the security posture of critical systems and applications after applying security patches, by integrating ethical hacking into vulnerability management processes, organizations can ensure that security vulnerabilities are effectively identified, prioritized, and remediated, furthermore, organizations can use ethical hacking techniques to supplement automated vulnerability scanning tools and techniques, while automated scanning tools are useful for identifying known vulnerabilities and misconfigurations, ethical hackers can leverage their creativity, expertise, and intuition to identify complex or obscure security vulnerabilities that may be overlooked by automated tools, for example, they can use manual penetration testing techniques, such as manual code review or fuzzing, to identify logic flaws or zero-day vulnerabilities in custom-built applications, by combining automated scanning with manual ethical hacking techniques, organizations can achieve a more comprehensive and accurate assessment of their security posture, additionally, organizations can integrate ethical hacking into their incident response processes by using ethical hackers to simulate real-world cyber attacks and assess the organization's ability to detect, respond to, and recover from security incidents, for example, they can conduct red team exercises to simulate targeted cyber attacks and assess the organization's detection and response capabilities, by incorporating ethical hacking into incident response processes, organizations can identify gaps in their security defenses and improve their incident response readiness, overall, integrating ethical hacking into vulnerability analysis processes is essential for enhancing the effectiveness, efficiency, and comprehensiveness of security assessments, organizations can leverage ethical hacking techniques and methodologies to identify, prioritize, and mitigate security vulnerabilities effectively, mitigate risks, and improve their overall security posture.

BOOK 3

CERTIFIED ETHICAL HACKER
MASTERING SOCIAL ENGINEERING TACTICS

ROB BOTWRIGHT

Chapter 1: Introduction to Social Engineering in Ethical Hacking

Social engineering in cybersecurity encompasses a range of psychological manipulation techniques used by attackers to exploit human vulnerabilities and gain unauthorized access to sensitive information or systems, one common social engineering technique is phishing, where attackers use deceptive emails, messages, or websites to trick individuals into divulging confidential information, such as login credentials or financial details, organizations can use email security solutions, such as Microsoft Exchange Online Protection (EOP) or Proofpoint, to detect and block phishing emails, for example, they can use the 'eop' command to configure email protection policies and settings in Microsoft Exchange Online Protection, another social engineering technique is pretexting, where attackers create a false pretext or scenario to manipulate individuals into disclosing information or performing actions they would not normally do, organizations can mitigate the risk of pretexting by implementing policies and procedures that require employees to verify the identity of individuals before disclosing sensitive information or fulfilling requests, for example, they can use the 'pretexting' command to create and enforce pretexting prevention policies, moreover, baiting is another social engineering technique where attackers offer something of value, such as a USB drive or a free download, to entice individuals into performing a specific action, such as inserting the USB drive into their computer or clicking on a malicious link, organizations can educate employees about the risks of baiting and implement security controls, such as endpoint protection software, to detect and block malicious USB devices or files, for example, they can use the 'endpointprotection' command to deploy and configure endpoint protection policies, furthermore, quid pro quo is a social engineering technique where attackers offer something in exchange for information or assistance, such as technical support or access to exclusive content, organizations can train employees to recognize and report suspicious requests for information or assistance and implement controls, such as access controls and user permissions, to limit the impact of quid pro quo attacks, for example, they can use the 'accesscontrols' command to configure user permissions and access controls, additionally, tailgating or piggybacking is a social engineering technique where attackers follow authorized individuals into secure areas or facilities without proper authentication, organizations can mitigate the risk of tailgating by implementing physical security measures, such as access control systems, security guards, and surveillance cameras, for example, they can use the 'accesscontrolsystems' command to configure and manage access control systems, overall, social engineering is a significant threat to organizations' cybersecurity posture, as attackers exploit human psychology and trust to bypass technical security controls, organizations can defend against social engineering attacks by educating employees about common social engineering techniques and implementing a layered approach to security that includes technical controls, policies, and procedures. The role and significance of social engineering in ethical hacking are paramount, as it encompasses a broad spectrum of techniques and tactics that ethical hackers employ to assess the security posture of organizations and systems, social engineering plays a critical role in ethical hacking by allowing testers to evaluate not only technical vulnerabilities but also human vulnerabilities within an organization, one of the primary goals of ethical hacking is to identify and mitigate security risks, and social engineering provides a unique perspective by focusing on the human element of security, ethical hackers use social engineering techniques to simulate real-world attacks and assess an organization's susceptibility to social manipulation and exploitation, for example, they can use the 'socialengineering' command to simulate social engineering attacks and measure the effectiveness of security awareness training programs, moreover, social engineering helps ethical hackers understand the psychology behind human behavior and decision-making, allowing them to craft more effective and convincing attack scenarios, ethical hackers leverage social engineering to gain unauthorized access to sensitive information or systems, bypassing technical controls and defenses, for example, they can use pretexting to deceive employees into disclosing their login credentials or access codes, furthermore, social engineering plays a significant role in red team exercises, where ethical hackers simulate advanced cyber attacks to test an organization's defenses, red teamers use social engineering tactics to infiltrate networks, compromise systems, and achieve their objectives, for example, they can use the 'redteam' command to conduct red team exercises that include social engineering components, additionally, social engineering is often used in penetration testing engagements to assess the effectiveness of an organization's security awareness training programs and policies, penetration testers use social engineering techniques to exploit human vulnerabilities and gain access to sensitive information or systems, for example, they can use phishing emails or phone calls to trick employees into revealing confidential information or clicking on malicious links, organizations can deploy security controls and measures to defend against social engineering attacks, such as implementing security awareness training programs, conducting simulated phishing exercises, and enforcing strict access controls, for example, they can use the 'securityawareness' command to deploy security awareness training modules and track employee progress, overall, social engineering is an essential component of ethical hacking, allowing testers to assess and improve an organization's overall security posture by identifying and mitigating human vulnerabilities, ethical hackers must use social engineering techniques responsibly and ethically, ensuring that their activities are conducted with the organization's consent and in compliance with applicable laws and regulations.

Chapter 2: Psychological Principles Behind Social Engineering

Understanding psychological triggers and influences is crucial in various fields, including marketing, sales, and cybersecurity, as it provides insights into human behavior and decision-making processes, one key aspect of understanding psychological triggers is recognizing the role of emotions in shaping behavior, emotions such as fear, curiosity, and desire can significantly influence how individuals respond to stimuli and make decisions, for example, in cybersecurity, attackers often exploit fear by creating urgent or threatening messages to prompt users to take immediate action, such as clicking on a malicious link or revealing sensitive information, organizations can deploy security awareness training programs to educate employees about common psychological triggers used in social engineering attacks and how to recognize and respond to them effectively, for example, they can use the 'securityawareness' command to deploy simulated phishing exercises that mimic real-world social engineering attacks, moreover, understanding cognitive biases is essential for recognizing and mitigating vulnerabilities in decision-making processes, cognitive biases are systematic patterns of deviation from rationality or logic in judgment, individuals may rely on cognitive shortcuts or heuristics to make decisions, which can lead to errors in judgment or decision-making, for example, confirmation bias is a cognitive bias where individuals seek out information that confirms their existing beliefs or hypotheses while ignoring or dismissing contradictory evidence, attackers can exploit confirmation bias by tailoring their messages to align with individuals' preconceived notions or beliefs, organizations can mitigate the impact of cognitive biases by implementing decision-making frameworks and processes that promote critical thinking and objectivity, for example, they can use the 'decisionmakingframework' command to establish decision-making protocols that encourage employees to consider multiple perspectives and evaluate evidence objectively, furthermore, understanding the principles of persuasion is essential for influencing behavior and attitudes, persuasion techniques such as reciprocity, scarcity, and authority can be used to motivate individuals to take specific actions or adopt certain beliefs, in cybersecurity, ethical hackers can leverage persuasion techniques to encourage employees to adhere to security policies and best practices, for example, they can use the 'persuasion' command to design security awareness campaigns that highlight the benefits of following security guidelines, additionally, understanding social norms and conformity is crucial for predicting and influencing group behavior, individuals may conform to social norms or group pressure to fit in or avoid social disapproval, attackers can exploit social norms by creating a sense of urgency or social proof to prompt individuals to comply with their requests, organizations can promote a culture of security by fostering a sense of collective responsibility and accountability among employees, for example, they can use the 'securityculture' command to assess and improve the organization's security culture through training, communication, and recognition programs, overall, understanding psychological triggers and influences is essential for effectively managing risks and shaping behavior in various contexts, organizations can leverage this knowledge to enhance security awareness, promote positive behaviors, and mitigate the impact of social engineering attacks. Psychological models play a pivotal role in understanding and executing social engineering tactics effectively, one widely recognized psychological model used in social engineering is the 'AIDA' model, which stands for Attention, Interest, Desire, and Action, this model outlines the steps involved in persuading individuals to take a specific action, such as clicking on a malicious link or disclosing sensitive information, ethical hackers can leverage the AIDA model to craft convincing social engineering messages that capture the target's attention, pique their interest, evoke desire, and prompt them to take action, for example, they can use the 'AIDA' command to structure their social engineering campaigns based on this model, another influential psychological model used in social engineering is the 'Foot-in-the-Door' technique, this technique relies on the principle of consistency, individuals are more likely to comply with a larger request if they have already agreed to a smaller one, attackers can exploit this principle by making a small initial request, such as completing a survey or signing up for a free trial, before making a larger request, such as providing login credentials or financial information, organizations can mitigate the effectiveness of the Foot-in-the-Door technique by educating employees about the tactics used in social engineering attacks and encouraging them to verify requests from unfamiliar or suspicious sources, additionally, the 'Authority' principle, as described by psychologist Robert Cialdini, suggests that individuals are more likely to comply with requests from authority figures or credible sources, attackers can exploit this principle by impersonating authority figures, such as IT administrators or company executives, to persuade individuals to comply with their requests, organizations can combat this tactic by implementing strict access controls and authentication mechanisms to verify the identity of individuals making requests for sensitive information or actions, moreover, the 'Scarcity' principle highlights the tendency for individuals to place a higher value on items or opportunities that are perceived as scarce or limited, attackers can leverage this principle by creating a sense of urgency or scarcity to prompt individuals to take immediate action, such as clicking on a link to avoid missing out on a limited-time offer or opportunity, organizations can mitigate the impact of the Scarcity principle by educating employees about common social engineering tactics and encouraging them to verify the legitimacy of requests before taking action, furthermore, social engineers often rely on principles of social proof and reciprocity to influence behavior, social proof refers to the tendency for individuals to look to others for guidance on how to behave in uncertain situations, attackers can exploit social proof by creating fake social media profiles or testimonials to validate their claims or requests, while reciprocity involves the tendency for individuals to feel obligated to reciprocate favors or gifts, attackers can use this principle by offering small gifts or incentives to individuals in exchange for compliance with their requests, organizations can counter these tactics by promoting a culture of skepticism and critical thinking, encouraging employees to question and verify requests before complying, overall, understanding and applying psychological models in social engineering is essential for ethical hackers to craft persuasive and convincing attack scenarios, as well as for organizations to develop effective defenses and countermeasures against social engineering attacks.

Chapter 3: Pretexting: Crafting Believable Scenarios

Crafting convincing pretexts is a crucial aspect of social engineering, as it involves creating believable scenarios or stories to manipulate individuals into disclosing sensitive information or performing certain actions, one effective technique for crafting convincing pretexts is to gather intelligence about the target organization and its employees, this can include researching the company's structure, culture, and key personnel, as well as gathering information from public sources such as social media profiles and online forums, armed with this knowledge, social engineers can tailor their pretexts to align with the target's interests, concerns, and daily routines, for example, they can use the 'osint' command to conduct open-source intelligence gathering to collect information about the target organization and its employees, another technique is to leverage social engineering principles such as authority and urgency to enhance the credibility of the pretext, social engineers can pose as trusted individuals, such as IT support personnel or company executives, to increase the likelihood of compliance with their requests, they can also create a sense of urgency or importance to prompt immediate action, such as claiming that a system update is required to prevent a security breach or that sensitive information needs to be verified for regulatory compliance purposes, to deploy this technique, social engineers can use the 'authority' and 'urgency' commands to establish their credibility and create a sense of urgency in their pretext, furthermore, social engineers can use persuasion techniques such as reciprocity and social proof to increase the effectiveness of their pretexts, for example, they can offer small favors or incentives to the target in exchange for compliance with their requests, or they can provide fake testimonials or references to validate their claims, by deploying these persuasion techniques, social engineers can make their pretexts more compelling and persuasive, organizations can mitigate the effectiveness of pretexting by implementing security awareness training programs that educate employees about common social engineering tactics and how to recognize and respond to them effectively, for example, they can use the 'securityawareness' command to deploy simulated phishing exercises that simulate real-world pretexting scenarios, this allows employees to practice identifying and mitigating social engineering attacks in a controlled environment, additionally, organizations can implement policies and procedures that require employees to verify requests for sensitive information or actions, such as requiring multi-factor authentication for access to sensitive systems or mandating the use of secure channels for communication, by establishing clear guidelines and protocols for handling requests, organizations can reduce the risk of falling victim to pretexting attacks, overall, crafting convincing pretexts requires a combination of research, social engineering principles, and persuasion techniques, social engineers must gather intelligence about the target organization and its employees, leverage social engineering principles to enhance the credibility of their pretexts, and use persuasion techniques to increase their effectiveness, while organizations can mitigate the risk of pretexting attacks by implementing security awareness training programs, policies, and procedures that educate employees about social engineering tactics and how to respond to them appropriately. Creating effective pretexting scenarios for social engineering involves a strategic approach to crafting believable and persuasive narratives that manipulate individuals into disclosing sensitive information or performing desired actions, one essential aspect of creating effective pretexting scenarios is conducting thorough research to gather intelligence about the target organization, its employees, and the context in which the social engineering attack will take place, this research phase often begins with open-source intelligence (OSINT) gathering, where social engineers collect information from publicly available sources such as company websites, social media platforms, online forums, and news articles, by analyzing this information, social engineers can identify potential entry points, vulnerabilities, and targets within the organization, they can use tools like Maltego or theHarvester to automate the process of gathering information from various online sources, allowing them to quickly identify key individuals, departments, and relationships within the target organization, armed with this intelligence, social engineers can tailor their pretexting scenarios to align with the target's interests, concerns, and daily routines, increasing the likelihood of success, for example, if the target organization is known for its commitment to environmental sustainability, a social engineer might craft a pretext around a fake charity initiative aimed at supporting eco-friendly causes, this pretext could involve soliciting donations or participation in a volunteer event under the guise of promoting corporate social responsibility, to further enhance the credibility of the pretext, social engineers can leverage principles of authority and urgency, posing as trusted individuals such as IT support personnel or company executives to increase the perceived legitimacy of their requests, they can also create a sense of urgency or importance to prompt immediate action, such as claiming that a critical system update is required to prevent a security breach or that sensitive information needs to be verified for regulatory compliance purposes, to deploy this technique, social engineers can use tools like SET (Social Engineering Toolkit) to generate phishing emails or conduct voice-based social engineering attacks (vishing) that exploit principles of authority and urgency, by impersonating trusted individuals and creating a sense of urgency, social engineers can increase the likelihood of compliance with their requests, however, it's essential to remember that effective pretexting is not just about deceiving the target, but also about building rapport and establishing trust, social engineers must use persuasive language and communication skills to engage the target in a meaningful way, building rapport and establishing trust takes time and patience, social engineers must invest the effort to develop a rapport with the target before attempting to manipulate them into disclosing sensitive information or performing desired actions, they can do this by demonstrating empathy, active listening, and a genuine interest in the target's concerns and needs, by building rapport and establishing trust, social engineers can create a psychological connection with the target, making them more susceptible to manipulation, however, it's crucial to note that pretexting scenarios must be ethical and legal, social engineers should never engage in activities that could cause harm or violate the law, this includes obtaining unauthorized access to systems or networks, stealing personal or confidential information, or engaging in fraudulent activities, social engineers must adhere to ethical guidelines and respect the privacy and rights of individuals and organizations, to ensure compliance with ethical and legal standards, organizations can implement policies and procedures that govern the use of social engineering tactics and provide clear guidelines for employees on how to recognize and respond to pretexting attempts, they can also provide security awareness training programs that educate employees about the dangers of social engineering attacks and how to protect themselves and the organization from potential threats, by promoting a culture of security awareness and ethical behavior, organizations can reduce the risk of falling victim to pretexting attacks and protect their sensitive information and assets from harm.

Chapter 4: Influence and Persuasion Techniques

Influencing and persuading targets is a critical skill in the realm of social engineering, requiring a deep understanding of human psychology and effective communication strategies, one technique commonly used by social engineers is the principle of reciprocity, which involves offering something of value to the target in exchange for compliance with the attacker's requests, this could be in the form of a small favor, a token gift, or helpful information, by initiating a reciprocal exchange, social engineers can create a sense of indebtedness in the target, making them more likely to reciprocate with a favorable response, another influential technique is the principle of authority, which leverages people's tendency to defer to individuals perceived as experts or figures of authority, social engineers can exploit this principle by posing as trusted professionals, such as IT technicians, security consultants, or company executives, to increase the likelihood of compliance with their requests, they can also use authoritative language and demeanor to convey confidence and credibility, thereby reinforcing their perceived expertise and legitimacy, for instance, a social engineer might impersonate a network administrator and instruct an employee to provide their login credentials for security verification purposes, exploiting the target's trust in authority figures to obtain sensitive information, social engineers can also employ the principle of scarcity, which capitalizes on people's fear of missing out on valuable opportunities or resources, by framing their requests in terms of limited availability or urgency, social engineers can create a sense of scarcity that motivates targets to act quickly and decisively, for example, they might claim that a special promotion or discount is about to expire, prompting the target to make an impulsive decision to take advantage of the offer, to deploy these techniques effectively, social engineers must carefully plan their approach and tailor their messaging to resonate with the target's motivations, concerns, and psychological triggers, they must also be adept at adapting their tactics in real-time based on the target's responses and behavior, one powerful persuasion technique is storytelling, which involves framing the attacker's requests within a narrative context that engages the target emotionally and psychologically, by telling a compelling story that highlights the benefits of compliance and the consequences of refusal, social engineers can capture the target's attention and elicit a more favorable response, for instance, they might create a scenario in which the target's actions are portrayed as heroic or altruistic, appealing to their sense of pride and moral obligation, to enhance the effectiveness of storytelling, social engineers can use vivid imagery, sensory language, and relatable characters to make the narrative more engaging and persuasive, they can also incorporate social proof, which involves referencing social norms, testimonials, or endorsements to validate the legitimacy of their requests and reassure the target that others have already complied, for example, they might mention that several colleagues have already participated in a company-wide initiative or that a respected industry leader has endorsed their proposal, increasing the perceived credibility and desirability of the request, by combining these techniques with careful planning, observation, and adaptation, social engineers can significantly increase their chances of success in influencing and persuading targets to disclose sensitive information, grant access to restricted resources, or perform desired actions, however, it's important to remember that these techniques must be used ethically and responsibly, social engineers should never manipulate or deceive individuals for malicious purposes or personal gain, instead, they should focus on raising awareness about the dangers of social engineering and helping organizations strengthen their defenses against potential threats, by promoting a culture of skepticism, critical thinking, and vigilance, organizations can empower employees to recognize and resist manipulation attempts, reducing the risk of falling victim to social engineering attacks and safeguarding sensitive information and assets from harm. Social engineering, as a discipline, relies heavily on understanding and leveraging psychological principles to influence human behavior, one key psychological strategy is the principle of reciprocity, wherein individuals feel compelled to reciprocate favors or gestures, in social engineering, this can be applied by offering something of perceived value to the target, such as assistance or information, which may increase the likelihood of compliance with the attacker's requests, a classic example of this is when an attacker offers to help a target with a task or provides them with seemingly helpful information, creating a sense of indebtedness that can be exploited to gain further cooperation, another psychological strategy is the principle of authority, which involves exploiting people's tendency to defer to figures of authority or expertise, social engineers can leverage this by posing as trusted professionals or authoritative figures, such as IT technicians or company executives, to increase compliance with their requests, they may use authoritative language and demeanor to convey confidence and legitimacy, thereby enhancing their perceived credibility and persuasiveness, for example, an attacker might impersonate a network administrator and instruct an employee to reset their password for security reasons, exploiting the target's trust in authority figures to obtain sensitive information, social engineers also frequently utilize the principle of scarcity, which capitalizes on people's fear of missing out on valuable opportunities or resources, by framing their requests in terms of limited availability or urgency, they can create a sense of scarcity that motivates targets to act quickly and decisively, for instance, they might claim that a special promotion or discount is about to expire, prompting the target to make an impulsive decision to take advantage of the offer, storytelling is another powerful psychological strategy used in social engineering, it involves framing the attacker's requests within a narrative context that engages the target emotionally and psychologically, by telling a compelling story that highlights the benefits of compliance and the consequences of refusal, social engineers can capture the target's attention and elicit a more favorable response, for example, they might create a scenario in which the target's actions are portrayed as heroic or altruistic, appealing to their sense of pride and moral obligation, to enhance the effectiveness of storytelling, social engineers can use vivid imagery, sensory language, and relatable characters to make the narrative more engaging and persuasive, they may also incorporate social proof, which involves referencing social norms, testimonials, or endorsements to validate the legitimacy of their requests and reassure the target that others have already complied, increasing the perceived credibility and desirability of the request, for example, they might mention that several colleagues have already participated in a company-wide initiative or that a respected industry leader has endorsed their proposal, social engineers must be adept at adapting their tactics based on the target's responses and behavior, carefully tailoring their approach to resonate with the target's motivations, concerns, and psychological triggers, this requires keen observation, empathy, and flexibility, as well as the ability to think on their feet and adjust their strategy in real-time, overall, successful social engineering relies on a deep understanding of human psychology and effective communication strategies, by leveraging psychological principles such as reciprocity, authority, scarcity, storytelling, and social proof, social engineers can increase their chances of influencing and persuading targets to disclose sensitive information, grant access to restricted resources, or perform desired actions, however, it's crucial to use these techniques ethically and responsibly, avoiding manipulation or deception for malicious purposes, instead, social engineers should focus on raising awareness about the dangers of social engineering and helping organizations strengthen their defenses against potential threats, by promoting a culture of skepticism, critical thinking, and vigilance, organizations can empower employees to recognize and resist manipulation attempts, reducing the risk of falling victim to social engineering attacks and safeguarding sensitive information and assets from harm.

Chapter 5: Building Rapport and Establishing Trust

Building rapport is a foundational skill in social engineering, enabling attackers to establish trust and credibility with their targets, this is essential for gaining cooperation and eliciting sensitive information or actions, one effective way to build rapport is through active listening, by demonstrating genuine interest in the target's concerns, opinions, and experiences, social engineers can create a sense of connection and empathy, fostering rapport and mutual understanding, active listening involves giving the target your full attention, maintaining eye contact, nodding in agreement, and paraphrasing their statements to show that you understand and value their perspective, for example, a social engineer might engage the target in a conversation about their hobbies or interests, actively listening to their responses and asking follow-up questions to deepen the conversation, another important aspect of building rapport is mirroring and matching, this involves subtly mimicking the target's body language, speech patterns, and mannerisms to create a sense of familiarity and rapport, for instance, if the target speaks slowly and gestures with their hands, the social engineer might adopt a similar pace and use similar gestures to establish rapport and build trust, mirroring and matching should be done subtly and gradually, to avoid appearing overly contrived or insincere, as this can undermine rapport and credibility, empathy is also critical for building rapport, by showing empathy for the target's emotions and experiences, social engineers can build trust and rapport, for example, if the target expresses frustration or concern about a problem they're facing, the social engineer might acknowledge their feelings and offer understanding and support, demonstrating empathy helps to create a sense of connection and mutual respect, which can make the target more receptive to the social engineer's requests or suggestions, establishing common ground is another effective way to build rapport, by finding shared interests, experiences, or values, social engineers can create a sense of camaraderie and rapport with the target, for example, if the social engineer discovers that they share a hobby or belong to the same professional association as the target, they can use this common ground as a basis for building rapport and establishing trust, reciprocity is also important for building rapport, by offering something of value to the target, such as assistance, information, or validation, social engineers can create a sense of indebtedness and goodwill, which can increase the target's willingness to cooperate and comply with their requests, for example, a social engineer might offer to help the target solve a problem or provide them with useful information, fostering a sense of reciprocity and mutual benefit, overall, building rapport is essential for successful social engineering, by demonstrating active listening, mirroring and matching, empathy, establishing common ground, and reciprocity, social engineers can create a sense of trust and connection with their targets, increasing the likelihood of achieving their objectives, however, it's important to use rapport-building techniques ethically and responsibly, avoiding manipulation or deception for malicious purposes, instead, social engineers should focus on building genuine relationships based on trust, respect, and mutual understanding, fostering a culture of openness and collaboration that benefits both parties. Establishing trust with targets is a fundamental aspect of social engineering, as it allows attackers to gain access to sensitive information or resources, one strategy for establishing trust is to create a convincing pretext, this involves crafting a believable scenario or identity that aligns with the target's expectations and experiences, for example, a social engineer posing as a technical support technician might use familiar terminology and reference common issues to create a sense of authenticity, another strategy is to leverage social proof, this involves providing evidence or testimonials that demonstrate the social engineer's credibility and expertise, for instance, a social engineer might mention previous successful interactions with colleagues or clients to establish trust with the target, demonstrating competence and reliability, building rapport is also essential for establishing trust, by actively listening to the target, mirroring their body language, and showing empathy, social engineers can create a sense of connection and understanding, fostering trust and cooperation, for example, a social engineer might engage the target in a conversation about their interests or concerns, actively listening to their responses and offering validation and support, fostering a sense of mutual respect and empathy, demonstrating empathy and understanding is another effective strategy for establishing trust, by acknowledging the target's feelings and experiences, social engineers can create a sense of empathy and rapport, fostering trust and cooperation, for instance, if the target expresses frustration or concern about a problem they're facing, the social engineer might offer understanding and support, validating their emotions and experiences, demonstrating consistency and reliability is also critical for establishing trust, by consistently delivering on promises and commitments, social engineers can demonstrate their trustworthiness and reliability, for example, if a social engineer promises to follow up with the target after a meeting, it's important to follow through on this commitment, demonstrating reliability and integrity, leveraging authority and expertise is another effective strategy for establishing trust, by positioning themselves as knowledgeable experts or authority figures, social engineers can create a sense of trust and respect with the target, for instance, a social engineer might cite relevant qualifications or experience to demonstrate their expertise, building credibility and trust, finally, fostering a sense of reciprocity and mutual benefit is essential for establishing trust, by offering something of value to the target, such as assistance, information, or validation, social engineers can create a sense of indebtedness and goodwill, which can increase the target's willingness to cooperate and comply with their requests, for example, a social engineer might offer to share useful information or resources with the target, fostering a sense of reciprocity and mutual benefit, overall, establishing trust with targets is essential for successful social engineering, by creating convincing pretexts, leveraging social proof, building rapport, demonstrating empathy and understanding, consistency and reliability, leveraging authority and expertise, and fostering reciprocity and mutual benefit, social engineers can create a sense of trust and cooperation with their targets, increasing the likelihood of achieving their objectives.

Chapter 6: Phishing and Email Spoofing

Phishing attacks represent one of the most prevalent and insidious threats in the realm of cybersecurity, exploiting human psychology and trust to deceive unsuspecting users into divulging sensitive information or performing malicious actions, phishing attacks typically involve the use of deceptive emails, messages, or websites that mimic legitimate entities or services, tricking recipients into believing they are interacting with a trusted source, one common method of phishing is email phishing, where attackers send fraudulent emails posing as reputable organizations, such as banks, social media platforms, or online retailers, requesting sensitive information such as login credentials, financial details, or personal data, to deploy an email phishing attack, attackers often use automated tools or scripts to mass-send phishing emails to a large number of potential targets, crafting convincing messages with compelling subject lines and persuasive content to increase the likelihood of success, for instance, an attacker might send an email claiming that the recipient's account has been compromised and urging them to click on a link to verify their identity or reset their password, another variant of phishing is spear phishing, which targets specific individuals or organizations with highly personalized and tailored messages, using information gleaned from social media profiles, company websites, or previous data breaches to make the phishing attempt more convincing, for example, a spear phishing email might address the recipient by name and reference specific projects or colleagues to create a sense of familiarity and legitimacy, increasing the likelihood of success, in addition to email phishing, phishing attacks can also occur through other communication channels, such as text messages (SMS phishing or smishing) or phone calls (voice phishing or vishing), where attackers use similar tactics to deceive users and elicit sensitive information, for example, a smishing attack might involve sending a text message claiming that the recipient has won a prize or needs to update their account information, prompting them to click on a malicious link or call a fake customer support number, similarly, a vishing attack might involve a phone call from someone posing as a bank representative, requesting the recipient to provide their account details or transfer funds to a fraudulent account, phishing attacks can also leverage social engineering techniques to manipulate victims into taking specific actions, such as creating a sense of urgency or fear to prompt immediate response, for example, an attacker might claim that the recipient's account will be suspended unless they provide their login credentials within a short timeframe, exploiting their fear of losing access to important services, to mitigate the risk of phishing attacks, organizations and individuals must implement robust security measures and awareness training programs to educate users about the telltale signs of phishing and how to respond appropriately, for instance, users should be wary of unsolicited emails or messages requesting sensitive information, especially if they contain spelling or grammatical errors, generic greetings, or urgent demands, they should also verify the legitimacy of any requests by contacting the supposed sender through official channels or visiting their website directly, rather than clicking on links or downloading attachments from suspicious sources, furthermore, organizations can deploy email filtering and anti-phishing solutions to automatically detect and block phishing attempts, using techniques such as sender authentication, content analysis, and URL reputation checking to identify and quarantine malicious emails before they reach users' inboxes, likewise, user authentication mechanisms such as multi-factor authentication (MFA) can add an extra layer of security by requiring additional verification steps beyond the traditional username and password, making it more difficult for attackers to compromise accounts through phishing, moreover, ongoing security awareness training and simulated phishing exercises can help reinforce good security practices and empower users to recognize and report phishing attempts effectively, enabling organizations to proactively identify and mitigate potential threats, ultimately, combating phishing requires a multi-faceted approach that combines technical controls, user education, and organizational vigilance to stay one step ahead of the ever-evolving tactics employed by cybercriminals. Email spoofing, a deceptive technique used by malicious actors to forge the sender's email address and manipulate recipients into believing the message is from a legitimate source, is a prevalent threat in the realm of cybersecurity, typically, email spoofing involves altering the "From" field in an email header to make it appear as though the message originated from a trusted entity, such as a reputable organization or individual, enabling attackers to trick recipients into opening the email, clicking on malicious links, or divulging sensitive information, for instance, an attacker might spoof the email address of a bank, social media platform, or colleague to send fraudulent messages requesting login credentials, financial details, or other confidential data, to execute an email spoofing attack, attackers often use readily available tools or scripts that allow them to modify email headers and disguise their identity, one commonly used tool for email spoofing is Telnet, a command-line utility that enables users to establish a TCP connection to a remote server and interact with it using text-based commands, to spoof an email using Telnet, the attacker first opens a command prompt or terminal window and enters the following command to initiate a Telnet session with the target mail server: telnet <mail-server> 25, where "<mail-server>" is the hostname or IP address of the recipient's mail server and "25" is the standard SMTP (Simple Mail Transfer Protocol) port used for sending emails, once connected to the mail server, the attacker manually crafts a spoofed email by typing SMTP commands directly into the Telnet session, including the "MAIL FROM" and "RCPT TO" commands to specify the sender and recipient email addresses, respectively, and the "DATA" command to begin composing the email body, for example, the attacker might enter the following commands: MAIL FROM: <spoofed@email.com> RCPT TO:

<victim@email.com> DATA, followed by the content of the email, including the subject line, message body, and any attachments, after composing the email, the attacker terminates the message with a period (".") on a line by itself and sends it by typing

"QUIT" to close the Telnet session, this process allows attackers to send spoofed emails directly to the target's mail server without using a traditional email client, making it more difficult to trace the origin of the attack, to mitigate the risk of email spoofing, organizations can implement various security measures and best practices to detect and prevent fraudulent emails from reaching users, one common approach is to deploy email authentication mechanisms such as SPF (Sender Policy Framework),

DKIM (DomainKeys Identified Mail), and DMARC (Domain-based Message Authentication, Reporting, and Conformance), which help verify the authenticity of incoming emails and detect spoofed messages, for example, SPF allows domain owners to specify which mail servers are authorized to send emails on behalf of their domain by publishing a DNS (Domain Name System) TXT record containing a list of approved IP addresses, similarly, DKIM adds a digital signature to outgoing emails using asymmetric cryptography, allowing recipients to verify that the message has not been tampered with during transit, DMARC builds upon SPF and DKIM by providing additional policy and reporting features, allowing domain owners to specify how to handle emails that fail authentication checks and receive reports on email delivery and authentication status, another effective countermeasure against email spoofing is to implement email filtering and anti-spam solutions that can automatically detect and block suspicious messages based on various criteria, such as sender reputation, content analysis, and known phishing indicators, for instance, organizations can use spam filters to flag emails with spoofed or suspicious sender addresses, quarantine messages containing suspicious attachments or URLs, and perform real-time threat intelligence lookups to identify and block known malicious senders, furthermore, user education and awareness training are critical components of any email security strategy, as they empower users to recognize the signs of email spoofing and phishing attempts and respond appropriately, for example, users should be educated about the importance of verifying the authenticity of sender addresses, checking for spelling or grammatical errors, and avoiding clicking on links or downloading attachments from unknown or untrusted sources, they should also be encouraged to report any suspicious emails to their organization's IT or security team for further investigation and remediation, by combining technical controls, email authentication mechanisms, and user awareness training, organizations can strengthen their defenses against email spoofing and reduce the risk of falling victim to phishing attacks, ultimately, email spoofing remains a persistent and evolving threat in the cybersecurity landscape, requiring constant vigilance and proactive measures to detect and mitigate potential risks.

Chapter 7: Vishing: Voice-Based Social Engineering Attacks

Vishing, a form of social engineering that leverages voice communication technology to deceive individuals into divulging sensitive information or performing actions that compromise their security, is a prevalent threat in the realm of cybersecurity, typically, vishing attacks involve attackers posing as legitimate entities, such as financial institutions, government agencies, or tech support personnel, and contacting potential victims via phone calls or voicemail messages, the goal of these attacks is to elicit confidential information, such as account credentials, social security numbers, or financial data, from unsuspecting individuals through persuasion, manipulation, or intimidation tactics, vishing attacks often exploit human vulnerabilities and psychological triggers to gain the trust and cooperation of their targets, making them a potent threat in today's interconnected world, to execute a vishing attack, attackers may use various techniques and strategies to deceive their targets and achieve their objectives, one common method is to impersonate a trusted authority figure or service provider and create a sense of urgency or fear to compel the victim to act hastily, for example, the attacker might claim to be from a bank's fraud department and inform the victim that their account has been compromised or that unauthorized transactions have been detected, prompting the victim to provide sensitive information or follow instructions to "verify" their identity, another tactic used in vishing attacks is to spoof caller ID information to make it appear as though the call is originating from a legitimate source, such as a government agency or reputable company, this can trick recipients into answering the call or trusting the caller without question, even if they are suspicious of the request, furthermore, vishing attacks often exploit common human biases and cognitive shortcuts to manipulate victims' behavior and decision-making processes, for instance, attackers may use authority bias by claiming to be an official representative of a well-known organization or authority figure, such as a police officer or government official, to compel the victim to comply with their demands, they may also exploit reciprocity bias by offering fake rewards or incentives, such as gift cards or discounts, in exchange for the victim's cooperation, creating a sense of obligation or indebtedness, additionally, vishing attacks may employ social proof by referencing other individuals or organizations that have purportedly fallen victim to the same scam, to validate the legitimacy of the request and reassure the victim that they are not alone, in recent years, vishing attacks have become increasingly sophisticated and difficult to detect, thanks to advancements in voice synthesis technology, attackers can now create highly realistic voice recordings or deepfake audio clips that mimic the voices of real individuals, making it challenging for victims to distinguish between genuine and fraudulent calls, furthermore, vishing attacks often target vulnerable populations, such as the elderly or less tech-savvy individuals, who may be more susceptible to manipulation or coercion, due to lack of awareness or understanding of the risks, to mitigate the risk of vishing attacks, individuals and organizations can implement various security measures and best practices to protect themselves and their assets, one effective countermeasure is to educate users about the tactics and techniques used in vishing attacks and encourage them to remain vigilant and skeptical of unsolicited calls or requests for sensitive information, they should be advised to verify the identity of the caller by asking for their name, contact information, and organization affiliation, and independently verify this information through official channels before providing any personal or confidential data, furthermore, organizations can implement call screening and authentication mechanisms, such as interactive voice response (IVR) systems or voice biometrics, to verify the identity of callers and detect suspicious or fraudulent activity, they can also deploy anti-vishing solutions that analyze call patterns and behaviors to identify potential vishing attempts and block or flag them for further investigation, additionally, organizations should establish clear policies and procedures for handling sensitive information over the phone and provide regular training and awareness programs to educate employees about the risks of vishing attacks and how to respond appropriately, by adopting a proactive approach to vishing prevention and mitigation, individuals and organizations can better protect themselves against this pervasive and evolving threat, safeguarding their privacy, financial security, and reputation in the process. Voice-based social engineering, also known as vishing, poses a significant threat to individuals and organizations alike, leveraging the human element to deceive targets and extract sensitive information or illicit actions, vishing attacks often exploit psychological triggers and vulnerabilities to manipulate victims into divulging confidential data or performing actions that compromise their security, one common technique used in vishing attacks is impersonation, where attackers pose as trusted entities, such as financial institutions, government agencies, or technical support personnel, to gain the trust and cooperation of their targets, attackers may spoof caller ID information to make it appear as though the call is coming from a legitimate source, increasing the likelihood that the victim will answer the phone or comply with their requests, another technique used in vishing attacks is pretexting, where attackers create elaborate scenarios or stories to convince victims to disclose sensitive information or perform specific actions, for example, an attacker may claim to be from a bank's fraud department and inform the victim that their account has been compromised, urging them to provide personal information to verify their identity, furthermore, vishing attacks often exploit common human biases and cognitive shortcuts to manipulate victims' behavior and decision-making processes, such as authority bias, reciprocity bias, and social proof, to mitigate the risk of vishing attacks, individuals and organizations can implement various security measures and best practices to protect themselves and their assets, one effective countermeasure is to educate users about the tactics and techniques used in vishing attacks and encourage them to remain vigilant and skeptical of unsolicited calls or requests for sensitive information, they should be advised to verify the identity of the caller by asking for their name, contact information, and organization affiliation, and independently verify this information through official channels before providing any personal or confidential data, furthermore, organizations can implement call screening and authentication mechanisms, such as interactive voice response (IVR) systems or voice biometrics, to verify the identity of callers and detect suspicious or fraudulent activity, they can also deploy anti-vishing solutions that analyze call patterns and behaviors to identify potential vishing attempts and block or flag them for further investigation, additionally, organizations should establish clear policies and procedures for handling sensitive information over the phone and provide regular training and awareness programs to educate employees about the risks of vishing attacks and how to respond appropriately, by adopting a proactive approach to vishing prevention and mitigation, individuals and organizations can better protect themselves against this pervasive and evolving threat, safeguarding their privacy, financial security, and reputation in the process.

Chapter 8: Impersonation and Identity Theft

Impersonation, a common tactic in social engineering, involves portraying oneself as someone else to gain trust, extract information, or manipulate individuals or systems, attackers often impersonate authority figures, trusted colleagues, or service providers to exploit human vulnerabilities and bypass security measures, one technique used in impersonation is pretexting, where attackers create a plausible scenario or backstory to convince targets to disclose sensitive information or perform specific actions, for example, an attacker may impersonate a bank employee and claim to be conducting a routine security check, requesting the target's account details to verify their identity, another technique is phishing, where attackers impersonate legitimate entities, such as banks, social media platforms, or government agencies, in fraudulent emails or messages to trick recipients into clicking on malicious links or disclosing login credentials, furthermore, attackers may use voice-based impersonation, also known as vishing, to impersonate trusted individuals or organizations over the phone, manipulating targets into providing confidential information or transferring funds, to deploy a phishing attack, an attacker may use command-line tools such as "curl" or "wget" to send spoofed emails or messages containing malicious links or attachments, for example, they could use the following command to send a phishing email with a fake sender address: "curl -s -X POST -H 'From: spoofed@email.com' -H 'Content-Type: text/plain' -d 'Click this link to claim your prize!' https://malicious.site/send-email", moreover, attackers may use social engineering toolkits such as "Social-Engineer Toolkit (SET)" to automate the creation and deployment of phishing campaigns, allowing them to easily generate fake websites, emails, and messages that appear legitimate to unsuspecting targets, in addition to email and voice-based impersonation, attackers may also impersonate individuals or organizations on social media platforms to deceive targets and gain access to sensitive information or networks, they may create fake profiles or accounts that mimic those of real users or companies, using persuasive language and convincing imagery to establish credibility and trust with their intended victims, furthermore, attackers may use advanced techniques such as deepfake technology to impersonate individuals in video or audio recordings, creating highly realistic simulations that are difficult to detect, by leveraging machine learning algorithms and facial mapping techniques, attackers can manipulate footage of real people to say or do things they never actually did, increasing the effectiveness of their impersonation efforts, however, despite the sophistication of these techniques, there are several countermeasures that individuals and organizations can employ to protect themselves against impersonation attacks, these include educating users about the tactics and techniques used in impersonation attacks and encouraging them to verify the identity of unfamiliar or suspicious individuals before disclosing sensitive information, organizations can also implement multi-factor authentication (MFA) and access controls to prevent unauthorized access to sensitive systems and data, as well as conduct regular security awareness training and phishing simulations to help employees recognize and respond to impersonation attempts, furthermore, organizations can monitor their networks and systems for signs of unauthorized access or suspicious activity, using intrusion detection systems (IDS) and security information and event management (SIEM) tools to detect and mitigate impersonation attacks in real-time, by taking a proactive approach to security and implementing robust defenses, individuals and organizations can reduce the risk of falling victim to impersonation attacks, safeguarding their assets, data, and reputation from harm. Identity theft, a prevalent cybercrime, involves stealing someone's personal information to commit fraud or other illegal activities, attackers use various methods to obtain this information, including phishing, social engineering, malware, and data breaches, phishing attacks often involve sending fraudulent emails or messages impersonating legitimate organizations to trick recipients into disclosing sensitive information such as usernames, passwords, and credit card numbers, social engineering tactics exploit human vulnerabilities by manipulating individuals into revealing personal information or performing actions that compromise their security, for example, an attacker may impersonate a trusted colleague or service provider to gain access to sensitive data, malware such as keyloggers and spyware are used to steal personal information from infected devices, capturing keystrokes, browsing history, and other sensitive data without the user's knowledge, data breaches occur when attackers gain unauthorized access to databases or systems containing personal information, exploiting vulnerabilities or weak security controls to steal large quantities of data, to prevent identity theft, individuals and organizations can take several proactive measures to safeguard personal information and mitigate the risk of unauthorized access, one of the most effective prevention measures is to regularly monitor financial statements and credit reports for suspicious activity, detecting unauthorized transactions or accounts early can help minimize the damage caused by identity theft, individuals should also be cautious when sharing personal information online, avoiding public Wi-Fi networks and using secure websites with HTTPS encryption when transmitting sensitive data, strong, unique passwords should be used for each online account, and multi-factor authentication (MFA) should be enabled whenever possible to add an extra layer of security, organizations can implement robust cybersecurity policies and procedures to protect against identity theft, including employee training on security best practices and the importance of safeguarding sensitive information, regular security assessments and vulnerability scans can help identify and address potential weaknesses in systems and networks, reducing the risk of data breaches and unauthorized access, encryption technologies such as SSL/TLS can be used to secure data in transit, protecting it from interception and tampering by unauthorized parties, furthermore, organizations should have incident response plans in place to quickly detect and respond to security incidents, minimizing the impact of a potential data breach or identity theft incident, by taking proactive steps to protect personal information and mitigate the risk of identity theft, individuals and organizations can safeguard their assets and reputation from harm, reducing the likelihood of falling victim to cybercriminals and fraudsters.

Chapter 9: Physical Security Bypass Techniques

Bypassing physical security measures requires careful planning and execution, attackers often exploit human vulnerabilities and weaknesses in security protocols to gain unauthorized access to restricted areas or sensitive information, one common method for bypassing physical security measures is tailgating, where an attacker follows an authorized individual through a secured entrance without proper authentication, to prevent tailgating, organizations can implement access control systems with biometric authentication or require employees to use access cards or keys to enter secure areas, another method used by attackers is social engineering, where they manipulate individuals into granting them access to restricted areas by posing as trusted personnel or contractors, attackers may use pretexting or impersonation techniques to deceive security personnel or bypass security checkpoints, to mitigate the risk of social engineering attacks, organizations should provide comprehensive security awareness training to employees, teaching them to recognize and report suspicious behavior or unauthorized access attempts, physical security measures such as locks, alarms, and surveillance cameras are essential for protecting sensitive areas and assets from unauthorized access, however, these measures can be circumvented through various methods, for example, attackers may use lock picking tools or brute force techniques to bypass locks or security barriers, organizations should regularly inspect and maintain physical security equipment to ensure it is functioning properly and cannot be easily tampered with, physical security guards play a crucial role in preventing unauthorized access and deterring potential intruders, they should be trained to recognize suspicious behavior and respond appropriately to security threats, organizations can also use security guards to patrol sensitive areas and monitor access points, providing an additional layer of protection against physical security breaches, in some cases, attackers may exploit vulnerabilities in building infrastructure or facilities to gain unauthorized access to sensitive areas, for example, they may use structural weaknesses or maintenance access points to bypass security controls, organizations should conduct regular security assessments and audits of their physical infrastructure to identify and address potential vulnerabilities, implementing layered security measures can help organizations mitigate the risk of physical security breaches, by combining access control systems, surveillance cameras, security guards, and physical barriers, organizations can create multiple layers of defense to protect against unauthorized access and intrusion, regular security testing and evaluation are essential for identifying and addressing weaknesses in physical security measures, organizations should conduct penetration tests and vulnerability assessments to identify potential security gaps and develop remediation plans to address them, by taking a proactive approach to physical security, organizations can better protect their assets and reduce the risk of unauthorized access and security breaches. Physical security exploitation involves identifying and exploiting vulnerabilities in physical security measures to gain unauthorized access to protected areas or assets, one common technique used by attackers is lock picking, which involves manipulating lock mechanisms to bypass physical locks and gain entry to secured areas, attackers may use specialized lock picking tools such as lock picks, tension wrenches, and bump keys to defeat various types of locks, including padlocks, deadbolts, and cylinder locks, to mitigate the risk of lock picking attacks, organizations should use high-security locks that are resistant to picking, bumping, and other forms of covert entry, another technique used by attackers is bypassing access control systems, attackers may exploit weaknesses in access control systems to gain unauthorized access to secure areas, such as using brute force attacks to guess access codes or exploiting vulnerabilities in card readers or keypads, organizations can mitigate the risk of access control system attacks by implementing multi-factor authentication, using encryption to protect access credentials, and regularly updating access control software and firmware, physical security exploitation may also involve exploiting weaknesses in surveillance systems, attackers may disable or manipulate surveillance cameras to avoid detection while carrying out unauthorized activities, organizations can mitigate the risk of surveillance system attacks by using tamper-resistant cameras, encrypting video feeds, and implementing intrusion detection systems to alert security personnel to suspicious activity, social engineering is another common technique used by attackers to exploit physical security vulnerabilities, attackers may impersonate employees, contractors, or other trusted individuals to gain access to restricted areas or assets, organizations can mitigate the risk of social engineering attacks by implementing strict visitor management policies, providing security awareness training to employees, and conducting background checks on personnel and contractors, physical security exploitation often requires careful planning and reconnaissance, attackers may conduct surveillance of target facilities to identify security weaknesses, such as blind spots in surveillance camera coverage or vulnerabilities in perimeter fencing, organizations can mitigate the risk of reconnaissance attacks by monitoring for suspicious behavior, conducting regular security patrols, and implementing security awareness training for employees, in addition to using traditional physical security measures, organizations can also use technology to enhance their security posture, for example, biometric access control systems use fingerprint, iris, or facial recognition to authenticate individuals and grant access to secure areas, organizations can also use RFID technology to track assets and personnel within a facility, allowing them to quickly identify and respond to security breaches, physical security exploitation requires a multi-layered approach to defense, organizations should implement a combination of physical security measures, technology solutions, and security awareness training to protect against physical security threats, regular security assessments and audits can help organizations identify and address vulnerabilities in their physical security measures, allowing them to stay one step ahead of potential attackers.

Chapter 10: Insider Threats and Insider Attacks

Insider threats in social engineering refer to the risks posed by individuals within an organization who exploit their access, knowledge, or privileges to compromise security, one common type of insider threat is malicious insiders, who intentionally misuse their access to steal sensitive information, sabotage systems, or carry out other malicious activities, malicious insiders may include disgruntled employees, contractors, or business partners who have access to sensitive data or critical systems, organizations can mitigate the risk of malicious insiders by implementing access controls, monitoring user activity, and conducting regular security training and awareness programs, accidental insiders are another type of insider threat, accidental insiders inadvertently compromise security through careless or negligent actions, such as clicking on phishing emails, sharing passwords, or mishandling sensitive data, organizations can mitigate the risk of accidental insiders by implementing security policies and procedures, such as data classification, encryption, and secure data disposal practices, privileged users are a high-risk category of insider threats, privileged users have elevated access rights and permissions, which can be exploited to carry out sophisticated attacks, such as privilege escalation, data exfiltration, or unauthorized system changes, organizations can mitigate the risk of privileged user threats by implementing least privilege principles, regularly reviewing and auditing access rights, and monitoring privileged user activity, insider threats in social engineering often involve a combination of technical and psychological tactics, attackers may use social engineering techniques, such as phishing, pretexting, or impersonation, to manipulate insiders into disclosing sensitive information or performing unauthorized actions, organizations can mitigate the risk of insider threats by implementing security controls, such as multi-factor authentication, encryption, and user behavior analytics, detecting insider threats requires a proactive approach to monitoring and analyzing user activity, organizations should implement security information and event management (SIEM) systems to collect and analyze log data from across their IT infrastructure, allowing them to detect and respond to suspicious behavior in real-time, employee monitoring tools can also help organizations identify insider threats by tracking user activity, such as file access, email communication, and web browsing, organizations must balance the need to protect against insider threats with the need to respect employee privacy and trust, implementing insider threat detection and prevention measures requires collaboration between IT, security, human resources, and legal departments, organizations should develop comprehensive insider threat programs that include policies, procedures, and technologies for identifying, mitigating, and responding to insider threats, regular security awareness training and education can help employees recognize and report insider threats, fostering a culture of security and accountability within the organization, ultimately, protecting against insider threats requires a combination of technical controls, security best practices, and employee vigilance, organizations must continuously adapt and evolve their insider threat programs to address emerging threats and vulnerabilities, ensuring that they remain resilient in the face of evolving cybersecurity challenges. Insider attacks pose significant risks to organizations, with various scenarios in which insiders exploit their access and privileges for malicious purposes, one common insider attack scenario is data exfiltration, where insiders steal sensitive information and transfer it outside the organization, to mitigate the risk of data exfiltration, organizations can implement data loss prevention (DLP) solutions to monitor and control the movement of sensitive data, another insider attack scenario is privilege abuse, where insiders misuse their elevated access rights to carry out unauthorized actions, such as modifying system configurations or deleting critical data, to mitigate the risk of privilege abuse, organizations should implement least privilege principles, regularly review and audit access rights, and monitor privileged user activity, insider attacks can also involve sabotage, where insiders intentionally disrupt or damage systems, applications, or networks, to mitigate the risk of sabotage, organizations should implement security controls, such as intrusion detection and prevention systems (IDPS), and conduct regular security assessments and penetration tests, insider attacks may also involve insider trading, where insiders use confidential information for personal gain in financial markets, to mitigate the risk of insider trading, organizations should implement strict access controls, monitor and log access to sensitive financial information, and enforce policies prohibiting the use of insider information for personal gain, insider attacks can be difficult to detect and prevent, as insiders often have legitimate access to systems and data, making their malicious activities harder to distinguish from normal behavior, to improve detection and response to insider attacks, organizations should implement security monitoring and analytics tools that can identify suspicious behavior and anomalous activity, user behavior analytics (UBA) solutions can analyze patterns of user activity and identify deviations from normal behavior that may indicate insider threats, organizations should also conduct regular security awareness training and education for employees to raise awareness of insider threats and teach them how to recognize and report suspicious behavior, fostering a culture of security and accountability within the organization, collaboration between IT, security, human resources, and legal departments is essential for effectively mitigating insider attacks, organizations should develop and maintain comprehensive insider threat programs that include policies, procedures, and technologies for identifying, mitigating, and responding to insider threats, regular risk assessments and security audits can help organizations identify and prioritize insider attack risks, allowing them to allocate resources and implement appropriate controls to mitigate those risks, ultimately, mitigating insider attacks requires a multi-layered approach that combines technical controls, security best practices, and employee awareness and vigilance, organizations must remain vigilant and proactive in their efforts to detect, prevent, and respond to insider attacks, continuously monitoring and adapting their security posture to address evolving insider threat risks.

Chapter 11: Social Engineering Toolkit and Frameworks

Social engineering toolkits are powerful resources for security professionals and ethical hackers alike, providing a wide range of tools and techniques for conducting social engineering attacks, one of the most well-known and widely used social engineering toolkits is the Social Engineer Toolkit (SET), developed by TrustedSec, SET is an open-source Python-based toolkit that includes a variety of attack vectors and payloads for conducting social engineering attacks, such as phishing, spear phishing, and credential harvesting, SET simplifies the process of creating and executing social engineering attacks, offering pre-configured attack scenarios and customizable templates, to deploy SET, users can clone the toolkit's GitHub repository using the Git command, `git clone https://github.com/trustedsec/social-engineer-toolkit.git`, after cloning the repository, users can navigate to the SET directory and run the toolkit using the `setoolkit` command, `cd social-engineer-toolkit && ./setoolkit`, this launches the SET interactive console, where users can select and configure various attack modules, SET includes modules for creating phishing emails, malicious websites, and payloads, as well as tools for conducting reconnaissance and gathering intelligence on targets, another popular social engineering toolkit is the Metasploit Framework, which includes a wide range of modules for conducting both network and social engineering attacks, Metasploit is a powerful penetration testing platform that allows users to exploit vulnerabilities and gain unauthorized access to systems, the framework includes modules for generating malicious payloads, creating phishing websites, and conducting client-side attacks, Metasploit can be installed on various operating systems, including Linux, Windows, and macOS, users can install Metasploit using the following commands on Kali Linux, `apt update && apt install metasploit-framework`, once installed, users can launch Metasploit by running the `msfconsole` command, `msfconsole`, this opens the Metasploit console, where users can search for and load modules, configure options, and execute attacks, in addition to SET and Metasploit, there are numerous other social engineering toolkits available, each with its own set of features and capabilities, some other notable social engineering toolkits include BeEF (Browser Exploitation Framework), Evilginx, and King Phisher, BeEF is a powerful tool for exploiting web browser vulnerabilities and conducting client-side attacks, Evilginx is a sophisticated tool for intercepting and hijacking web sessions, while King Phisher is a versatile phishing toolkit with support for multi-stage campaigns and tracking, when using social engineering toolkits, it's important to remember ethical considerations and legal implications, social engineering attacks can have serious consequences and may violate laws and regulations, including privacy and data protection laws, therefore, it's essential to use these tools responsibly and ethically, only conducting social engineering attacks with proper authorization and consent, security professionals and ethical hackers should also take steps to protect themselves and their organizations from social engineering attacks, including implementing security awareness training programs, regularly updating security policies and procedures, and deploying security controls, such as email filtering, web filtering, and multi-factor authentication, by understanding the capabilities and limitations of social engineering toolkits, security professionals can better defend against social engineering attacks and protect their organizations from potential threats. Frameworks for conducting social engineering assessments are essential for organizing and guiding the process of assessing an organization's susceptibility to social engineering attacks, one widely used framework is the Open Source Security Testing Methodology Manual (OSSTMM), which provides a comprehensive and structured approach to security testing, including social engineering assessments, the OSSTMM defines various stages of assessment, such as information gathering, threat modeling, and vulnerability analysis, to deploy the OSSTMM framework, security professionals can download the methodology manual from the official website and follow the guidelines outlined in the manual, another popular framework for conducting social engineering assessments is the Penetration Testing Execution Standard (PTES), PTES is a comprehensive standard for performing penetration testing, including social engineering, the PTES framework defines seven phases of penetration testing, including pre-engagement interactions, intelligence gathering, and post-exploitation, to use the PTES framework, security professionals can download the standard from the official website and follow the guidelines provided, the Social Engineering Engagement Framework (SEEF) is another framework specifically tailored for social engineering assessments, SEEF provides a structured approach to planning, executing, and documenting social engineering engagements, the framework includes various templates, checklists, and guidelines for conducting social engineering assessments, to deploy the SEEF framework, security professionals can download the framework from the official website and customize it to meet their specific requirements, the SEEF framework covers all aspects of social engineering assessments, including reconnaissance, pretexting, and exploitation, yet another framework for conducting social engineering assessments is the Social Engineering Toolkit (SET), which was previously discussed as a toolkit but can also be used as a framework for organizing social engineering engagements, SET provides a modular and customizable approach to conducting social engineering assessments, allowing security professionals to select and configure various attack vectors and payloads, to use SET as a framework, security professionals can follow the guidelines provided in the documentation and adapt the toolkit's modules and payloads to their specific needs, the Common Attack Pattern Enumeration and Classification (CAPEC) framework is a comprehensive catalog of common attack patterns and techniques, including social engineering attacks, CAPEC provides detailed descriptions of each attack pattern, including potential impact, prerequisites, and countermeasures, to deploy CAPEC, security professionals can access the framework from the official website and use it as a reference when planning and executing social engineering assessments, finally, the NIST Special Publication 800-61, Revision 2, "Computer

Security Incident Handling Guide," provides guidelines for detecting, analyzing, and responding to security incidents, including social engineering attacks, the publication outlines a structured approach to incident handling, including preparation, detection, containment, eradication, and recovery, security professionals can use this publication as a framework for organizing their response to social engineering incidents, ensuring that they are handled effectively and efficiently.

Chapter 12: Mitigation Strategies and Countermeasures against Social Engineering

Effective mitigation strategies for social engineering attacks are crucial for organizations to safeguard their sensitive information and assets, one of the most fundamental strategies is employee training and awareness programs, which educate employees about the various social engineering tactics and how to recognize and respond to them, organizations can conduct regular training sessions, workshops, and simulations to ensure that employees are equipped with the knowledge and skills to identify and thwart social engineering attempts, implementing strong access controls and authentication mechanisms is another vital mitigation strategy, organizations should enforce the principle of least privilege, ensuring that employees only have access to the information and resources necessary for their job roles, multifactor authentication (MFA) should be implemented wherever possible to add an extra layer of security, deploying robust email security solutions can help prevent phishing attacks, organizations should use email filtering technologies to detect and block malicious emails containing phishing links or attachments, advanced email security solutions can also analyze email content and sender behavior to identify suspicious emails, implementing security policies and procedures is essential for establishing clear guidelines on how to handle sensitive information and respond to social engineering incidents, organizations should define policies for verifying the identity of unknown individuals requesting access to sensitive information or resources, establishing incident response plans and procedures is crucial for ensuring that social engineering incidents are promptly detected and effectively mitigated, organizations should develop detailed incident response plans that outline the steps to be taken in the event of a social engineering attack, including procedures for notifying appropriate personnel, containing the incident, and restoring normal operations, conducting regular security assessments and audits can help identify vulnerabilities and weaknesses that could be exploited by social engineering attacks, organizations should perform periodic vulnerability assessments and penetration tests to identify and remediate security gaps, implementing security controls such as data encryption, network segmentation, and intrusion detection systems (IDS) can help detect and mitigate social engineering attacks, organizations should encrypt sensitive data both at rest and in transit to prevent unauthorized access, network segmentation can limit the impact of social engineering attacks by isolating critical systems and resources from less sensitive areas of the network, IDS can monitor network traffic for signs of suspicious activity indicative of a social engineering attack, collaborating with industry peers and sharing threat intelligence can help organizations stay informed about emerging social engineering tactics and trends, organizations can join information sharing and analysis centers (ISACs) or other industry groups to exchange threat intelligence and best practices with other organizations in their sector, staying up-to-date with the latest security patches and updates is essential for mitigating social engineering attacks, organizations should regularly patch and update their software, operating systems, and security tools to address known vulnerabilities and weaknesses, implementing a robust security awareness program for employees, combined with strong access controls, email security solutions, security policies and procedures, incident response plans, security assessments and audits, security controls, threat intelligence sharing, and patch management, can significantly reduce the risk of falling victim to social engineering attacks. Implementing countermeasures to prevent social engineering incidents is critical in today's cybersecurity landscape, one effective countermeasure is to educate employees about the various social engineering techniques and tactics that attackers may use to manipulate them, this can be done through regular training sessions, workshops, and simulated phishing exercises, where employees are exposed to real-world scenarios and taught how to recognize and respond to suspicious emails, phone calls, and other forms of social engineering, providing employees with clear guidelines on how to handle sensitive information and how to verify the identity of individuals requesting access to such information can help prevent unauthorized disclosures, organizations should develop and enforce security policies and procedures that outline the proper protocols for handling sensitive data, such as requiring employees to verify the identity of unknown individuals before providing access to sensitive information, implementing strong access controls and authentication mechanisms is another essential countermeasure, organizations should enforce the principle of least privilege, ensuring that employees only have access to the information and resources necessary for their job roles, multifactor authentication (MFA) should be implemented wherever possible to add an extra layer of security, organizations should also deploy robust email security solutions to prevent phishing attacks, this includes using email filtering technologies to detect and block malicious emails containing phishing links or attachments, as well as implementing advanced email security solutions that can analyze email content and sender behavior to identify suspicious emails, implementing security controls such as data encryption, network segmentation, and intrusion detection systems (IDS) can help detect and mitigate social engineering attacks, organizations should encrypt sensitive data both at rest and in transit to prevent unauthorized access, network segmentation can limit the impact of social engineering attacks by isolating critical systems and resources from less sensitive areas of the network, IDS can monitor network traffic for signs of suspicious activity indicative of a social engineering attack, collaborating with industry peers and sharing threat intelligence can also help organizations stay informed about emerging social engineering tactics and trends, organizations can join information sharing and analysis centers (ISACs) or other industry groups to exchange threat intelligence and best practices with other organizations in their sector, staying up-to-date with the latest security patches and updates is essential for mitigating social engineering attacks, organizations should regularly patch and update their software, operating systems, and security tools to address known vulnerabilities and weaknesses, implementing a comprehensive security awareness program combined with strong access controls, email security solutions, security policies and procedures, security controls, threat intelligence sharing, and patch management can significantly reduce the risk of falling victim to social engineering attacks.

Conclusion

In summary, the "Certified Ethical Hacker: Reconnaissance, Vulnerability Analysis & Social Engineering" book bundle provides a comprehensive and practical guide for individuals aspiring to become skilled ethical hackers. Through the foundational knowledge offered in "Book 1 - Certified Ethical Hacker: Foundations of Reconnaissance Techniques," readers gain a solid understanding of the essential concepts and techniques used in reconnaissance, enabling them to gather critical information about target systems and networks. Building upon this groundwork, "Book 2 - Certified Ethical Hacker: Advanced Vulnerability Analysis Strategies" delves deeper into the intricacies of vulnerability analysis, equipping readers with advanced strategies for identifying and exploiting vulnerabilities in target systems. Finally, "Book 3 - Certified Ethical Hacker: Mastering Social Engineering Tactics" explores the human element of cybersecurity, providing readers with insights into the psychological triggers and manipulative tactics used in social engineering attacks.

By combining these three books, readers are not only equipped with the technical skills required for ethical hacking but also gain a comprehensive understanding of the multifaceted nature of cybersecurity threats. Through hands-on exercises, case studies, and real-world examples, the bundle empowers readers to apply ethical hacking techniques responsibly and ethically, helping organizations identify and remediate security vulnerabilities before malicious actors can exploit them.

Overall, the "Certified Ethical Hacker: Reconnaissance, Vulnerability Analysis & Social Engineering" book bundle serves as a valuable resource for cybersecurity professionals, students, and anyone interested in learning about the principles and practices of ethical hacking. Whether readers are looking to enhance their career prospects or bolster their organization's security posture, this bundle provides the knowledge and skills needed to succeed in the dynamic field of cybersecurity.